What's Your Wicca IQ?

What's Your Wicca IQ?

Laura A. Wildman, HPs

CITADEL PRESS
Kensington Publishing Corp.
www.kensingtonbooks.com

This book present information based upon the research and personal experiences of the author. It is not intended to be a substitute for a professional consultation with a physician or other health-care provider. Neither the publisher nor the author can be held responsible for any adverse effects or consequences resulting from the use of any of the information in this book. They also cannot be held responsible for any errors or omissions in the book. If you have a condition that requires medical advice, the publisher and authors urge you to consult a competent health-care professional.

CITADEL PRESS BOOKS are published by

Kensington Publishing Corp.
850 Third Avenue
New York, NY 10022

All Kensington titles, imprints, and distributed lines are available at special quantity discounts for bulk purchases for sales promotions, premiums, fundraising, and educational or institutional use. Special book excerpts or customized printings can also be created to fit specific needs. For details, write or phone the office of the Kensington special sales manager: Kensington Publishing Corp., 850 Third Avenue, New York, NY 10022, attn: Special Sales Department, phone: 1-800-221-2647.

CITADEL PRESS and the Citadel logo are Reg. U.S. Pat. & TM Off.

Designed by Leonard Telesca

First Printing: June 2002

10 9 8 7 6 5 4 3 2

Printed in the United States of America

Library of Congress Control Number: 2002100667

ISBN: 0-8065-2347-6

To Tom
my husband, partner, and friend,

whose loving support included many evenings spent alone on the
couch and serving me dinner at the computer
so that this book could be completed on time

and to the spirits of our children
whose presence in our lives we're looking forward to
with great joy

Contents

Acknowledgments

I wish to thank all my loving friends who helped to make this book possible.

Rene Cyr, who line edited the entire manuscript, giving me helpful comments and support. My Priestess and friend Judy Harrow, who kept me out of trouble and whose friendship I treasure! Alexei Kondratiev, for his knowledge on history and mythology. Len and Maria for helping me with the astrology section. Kaitlin Creed, Charles Boyce, and Jonathan, who helped fill in the gaps. Tracy for her herbal knowledge. Doug Nelson for his I Ching and Kabbalah insights. Kirk White, who knows a more about Ceremonial Magic and the Kabbalah than I'll ever want to and whose knowledge and stamina I admire. Mary Colleen and Ted for throwing a party to help come up with questions. Linda and the members of her coven for testing the first chapter to find the problems. The puppy pile and the attendees of Panthea who stayed up late in the cafeteria brainstorming with me. The members of Apple and Oak Coven, Geoff, Joan, Tim, Karyn, and Ijod, for their love and for understanding why their Priestess was often not available. And lastly Jenny Dunham, who called me with the idea to do this book and held my hand throughout the process.

Introduction

What is an athame? What is a Witch Queen? Samhain is a celebration of which holiday? When the Tower card appears in a Tarot reading, what might it be indicating? For what purpose would you burn the herb rue? When is a good time to work magic for healing? These are just a few of the questions offered in this book to challenge your Wiccan knowledge and magical skills.

The last twenty years have seen a major increase in the interest in Wicca, also called modern Witchcraft, the Craft, and Neo-Paganism. Wicca has been acknowledged as one the fastest-growing religions in North America. Current estimates place the numbers at approximately three to five million practicing either Wicca or some form of Paganism within a formal coven structure or on their own. Given the substantial numbers of teenagers who devoutly follow shows such as *Sabrina* and *Charmed*, and the number of national television shows—including *J.A.G.* and *Judging Amy*—that have either included a Pagan character or made it the topic for an episode, these numbers can only be increasing. In response to this rise in esoteric interest, and for better or worse, a plethora of Web sites, periodicals, and books has appeared on the market, all happily providing information on the Craft to those who seek it.

With all this knowledge flying around and easily accessible, how much Wicca wisdom and trivia have you managed to cram into your head or assimilate into your regular ritual practices and daily life? With so much stuff to learn, what has fallen between the proverbial cracks? The questions in this book cover a broad spectrum of information and levels of difficulty. Whether you are a beginner or have been practicing for years, it is designed to assess your current level of knowledge on Wicca and magical practice, identify your strengths, pinpoint areas for more study, and perhaps help open the door to adventure in realms previously not explored.

How to Use This Book

The general purpose of *What's Your Wicca I.Q.?* is to reaffirm your strengths and discover fields in which you may need further development. For this reason, the book has been broken down into six chapters, each containing very broad topics of general knowledge: beliefs, tools, history, spellcraft, divination, and Ceremonial Magic.

Each chapter is further divided into categories and subcategories that will help fine-tune your areas of expertise or ignorance. For example, chapter 1, "You Believe What?!" contains questions on general beliefs, vocabulary, Wiccan Traditions, and general mythology. You may find that you have a firm grasp on Wiccan vocabulary but know very little about the various Wiccan Traditions that created or currently make up the modern practices within the Craft. This gap in your training can easily be fixed by picking up a book or two on Wiccan history. Where possible, I've listed various sources you can turn to for more information.

Most of the questions are in a multiple-choice format. You will be offered a question and four possible answers from which to choose. Most questions are worth 2 points per correct answer, but there are a few mix and match lists that will be worth 1 point per correct match. For example:

1. Match each color association with its corresponding elements (1 point per correct match):

   a. red   _____   1. Earth
   b. blue   _____   2. Air
   c. yellow   _____   3. Water
   d. green   _____   4. Fire

Your answers versus the correct answers are listed at the end of the chapter:

ANSWERS

		Yours	Correct		
a.	Red	4	4	Fire	RIGHT = 1 point
b.	Blue	1	3	Water X	WRONG = 0 points
c.	Yellow	2	2	Air	RIGHT = 1 point
d.	Green	3	1	Earth X	WRONG = 0 points

Total points for question 1 = 2 points

In other words, question 1 had four possible correct matches. Each correct match was worth 1 point. If all the matches were correct, you would have received 4 points for the question. But in this example, out of those possible four, two of the matches were incorrect and two of the matches were right. This means you would receive only 2 out of the possible 4 points.

When taking this exam, you could circle your letter choice directly in the book, but instead I suggest you use a separate sheet of paper to keep track of the numbered questions and your selected answers. It will make it easier later when you compare your answers against those listed in the book. It will also give you an opportunity to retest yourself at a later date to see if you have strengthened skills over time.

Each section within a chapter is graded individually. The total points for each section are then added together at the end of the chapter to give you your final score for that chapter. It is these final scores that will be forwarded to the end of the book for your ultimate tally and assessment.

Unlike most I.Q. tests, where you are rushing against a clock, you can take as much time as you need to complete each chapter. If you are unsure of an answer, leave it and come back to it later.

Reviewing the Answers

The answers to each section are found at the end of its corresponding chapter. Nothing drives me crazier when taking an exam than getting an answer wrong with no explanation why my choice wasn't correct! I didn't want to make you experience this frustration, so I've included with most of the answers an explanation or supplemental information.

When using this book remember: Witches and Pagans are, in general, a very independent and opinionated lot. There are various ideas about is the "correct" way of doing things. Many of the questions in this book have been the topic of heated debates. Quite a few of the answers are subject to personal interpretation. The key is not whether you agree or disagree with my choice, but if you have an understanding of the underpinnings of your own selection.

Have fun with this book! Remember, no matter how long you have been practicing, you will always be a student: Learning never ends.

Want more *What's Your Wicca I.Q.?* Go to www.laurawildman. net.

You Believe What?!
Witches, Wiccans, Pagans, and Their Beliefs

There is a saying: "Ask three Witches for an opinion and you'll get eight answers." It isn't that Witches are confused or unsure about their beliefs but that Witches see the world as being multifaceted and multidimensional. As such, we realize it holds many truths and many possibilities, each of which is valid. There are no set dogmas within the Wiccan faith. We have no charismatic leader telling us the one true way. We have no Bible setting a canon of tradition. We often don't even worship the same Gods! We are an experiential religion that stresses individuality and self-expression, and honors the sacredness of the Earth and all who reside upon her.

But within the flexibility of Wicca, there are still characteristics that identify it and its members as practitioners of a particular religious faith. There is a recognizable format, a number of core beliefs, principles, ethics, and set of vocabulary used by the vast majority of Wiccans and Pagans. Notice I said *majority*. The questions and answers in this book were written for those who are within in this broad group. If you belong to one of the other crowds and you get a question wrong but firmly believe that, based upon your Tradition's practices or beliefs, your answer to the question is correct, please don't send me a flaming letter; just give yourself the point! This does not, however, give the rest of you carte blanche to pick your answers and call them all right just because you said so. Be honest with yourself. All of us are growing and learning. We are a very diverse group, and when I created these questions I tried to walk the centerline. Remember—have fun!

SECTION 1

Wicca and Witches

What is a Witch and how do you become one? What is Wicca? In order to begin, you need to know who and what we are.

1. Wicca is
   a. a modern Earth-based religion
   b. a dangerous cult
   c. a social movement
   d. all of the above

2. Wicca, or modern Witchcraft, is also called,
   a. Ancestral Rites
   b. the Ancient Way
   c. the Craft
   d. the Wiccan Way

3. A practitioner of Wicca is called a
   a. Wiccan
   b. Witch
   c. Follower
   d. Groupie

4. The origins of the Wiccan religious system can be traced back to
   a. the matriarchal cultures of the Stone Age
   b. the work of Gerald Gardner, Doreen Valiente, and others in the mid–twentieth century
   c. Alex Sanders's grandmother

    d. knowledge passed down from fragments of the lost city of Atlantis

5. From what word is the term *Wicca* derived?
    a. the Old English word *wican*, meaning "to bend"
    b. the Old English word *wis* or *wic*, meaning "wise"
    c. the Old English *wicce*, meaning "witch"
    d. unknown

6. The word *Pagan* comes from the Latin word *paganus*, meaning
    a. country dweller
    b. non-Christian
    c. Witch
    d. wise

7. The following adaptation of the word *Pagan* is often used to denote the differences between the Pagans of ancient history and those who follow a modern, reconstructed Pagan religion:
    a. modern Paganism
    b. contemporary Paganism
    c. new Paganism
    d. Neo-Paganism

8. Paganism, as a movement, is best described as
    a. highly structured, unified, and organized
    b. hierarchical in nature and narrow in its view of the world
    c. not unified, structured, or highly organized
    d. there is no such thing as a "Pagan movement"

9. What is magic?
    a. the art of changing consciousness and physical reality in accordance with will
    b. the connections and movements of energy
    c. conjuring tricks
    d. sleight of hand, juggling balls, pulling a rabbit out of a hat, and so forth

10. The primary differences between modern Witchcraft and
    that practiced by our ancestors are
    a. there are no differences between the past practice and the
       present practice
    b. ancient Witchcraft practices focused strictly on folk magic—
       the healer, the cunning man or woman—while modern
       Witchcraft is based primarily on ceremonial ritual
    c. there were no Witches prior to 1950s and the creation of
       Wicca
    d. modern Witchcraft is a combination of folk magic, Cere-
       monial Magic, bits of Pagan celebrations, and the occult

11. In general, _____ are _____, but not all _____ are _____ .
    a. Pagans, Witches; Witches, Pagans
    b. Witches, Pagans; Pagans, Witches
    c. Heathens, Asatru; Asatru, Heathens
    d. Shamans, Druids; Druids, Shamans

12. Witches are people who
    a. work in harmony with the energies of Nature and with
       their own magical abilities
    b. can foretell the future
    c. dance around bonfires and participate in sexual orgies
    d. work their will on others in order to facilitate change

13. Witches practice rites to attune themselves with
    a. the powers of the Gods for the purpose of obtaining
       wealth and success
    b. their coven and community
    c. the natural rhythms and cycles of life forces as marked by
       the phases of the moon
    d. all of the above

14. A Witch's magic and psychic abilities usually
    a. are hereditary
    b. are the self-development of natural instinct, which is de-
       rived from the natural potential found within everyone
    c. do not really exist
    d. are beamed down from outer space

15. How do you become a Witch?
    a. you must be born into a Witch family
    b. through initiation into a Wiccan coven
    c. by dedicating your life to attuning yourself to the ancient knowledge and ethics and ways as practiced in Wicca
    d. through the receiving of a prophetic dream or vision

16. How do you know when you have become a Witch?
    a. you receive in the mail a certificate suitable for framing
    b. your library has expanded threefold
    c. your Priestess tells you you are one
    d. you've made a heartfelt pledge to the Gods to follow the Wiccan ways and feel your commitment was accepted

SECTION 2

Walking the Walk and Talking the Talk— Beliefs and Vocabulary

We may be unique in our outlooks, but within Wicca there is a common core of beliefs and a vocabulary we use to describe our experiences. These commonalities are the things that help bind us together as a recognizable community.

17. A male Witch is called a
    a. Magus
    b. Warlock
    c. Witch
    d. Consort

18. A group of Witches who come together to practice their religion is
    a. a coven
    b. a unit
    c. a tribe
    d. a family

19. What is the difference between *immanent* and *eminent*?

a. nothing—one is the American spelling, the other British
b. one refers to the Divine that is within everything, the other means "distinguished" or "famous"
c. one means "happening," the other "waiting to happen"
d. one is the God found within, the other is God found outside of creation

20. Pantheism is
   a. a religious concept that identifies the Gods as present in all matter
   b. the worship or honoring of a collection of deities from the same culture
   c. the celebration and worship of the God Pan
   d. a famous temple in Greece dedicated to the Goddess Athena

21. Animism is
   a. a style of Japanese cartooning
   b. the acknowledgment of the spiritual consciousness of all elements of Nature
   c. the principle that like things are attracted to each other
   d. connecting with the animal consciousness within yourself

22. What is henotheism?
   a. the ritual application of henna to mark your devotion to a specific God or Goddess
   b. the totemic use of the chicken
   c. the dedication to and worship of the Goddess Hera
   d. the idea that you can worship a single deity without denying the existence of other deities

23. Hermeticisim is _____ , and its importance within Wicca is _____ .
   a. the dedication to the God Hermes; He is considered to be the God of the Witches
   b. a metaphysical and magical philosophy; it provided the basis of Ceremonial and Western occult magic
   c. a self-sufficient form of magic; it teaches the practitioner how to expunge all other thoughts

     d. a belief that centers on the healing of the inner self to help obtain balance and external abundance of material wealth; a primary magical philosophy

24. Polytheism is defined as
     a. the belief in, or worship of, more than one God or Goddess
     b. the practice of having more than one wife or husband
     c. the practice of having more than one sexual partner or relationship
     d. a new form of synthetic fiber

25. The following is a Sanskrit word that is used to describe the essence or spirit. It is sometimes also called *ether*, the emptiness from which reality takes its form:
     a. Rumi
     b. Tatoli
     c. Akasha
     d. Chakra

26. Also defined as the "original model," the following are personalities or sets of characteristics that are shared throughout all cultures. They give form to the myths and heroic stories that help express a culture's worldview:
     a. archetypes
     b. the Gods
     c. animism
     d. the Ancient Ones

27. Egregore would best be described as
     a. overexuberant in faith
     b. an ancient Greek text containing spells and rituals that modern Witches have adapted and used
     c. a type of music used to raise energy
     d. group mind or group energy

28. Elementals are best described as
     a. the four elements of life found within Nature, which form the foundation of natural magic

b. the spirits that personify the four elements
c. a Pagan music group that wrote many of the chants currently used within the Pagan community
d. earth, air, fire, and water

29. Not all Witches choose to work with a coven. Some prefer to worship as a
a. Strega
b. member of a tribe
c. solitary
d. Priest

30. This book is the "bible" of the Witches:
a. there is no such thing as a Witches' bible
b. *Drawing Down the Moon*, by Margot Adler
c. *The Spiral Dance*, by Starhawk
d. *Eight Sabbats for Witches*, by Janet and Stewart Farrar

31. The Wiccan Rede is a code of ethics that is universally recognized within the Wiccan and Pagan communities. It states
a. what energy you send out, for good or for ill, will come back to you threefold
b. do what thou wilt shall be the whole of the law
c. an it harm none, do what thou wilt
d. honor the God, Goddess, and Nature and walk in harmony with all

32. Derived from the Eastern philosophy of karma, this Wiccan belief has more to do with causality than law:
a. do what thou wilt shall be the whole of the law
b. the law of the Tao
c. the laws of magic
d. threefold law of return

33. The Charge of the Goddess is
a. Visa, MasterCard, MistressCard, or American Express
b. the Goddess's directions on how all Wiccan worship should be conducted

    c. an inspirational ritual poem

    d. an encoded message understood only by the initiate

34. The Eleusinian mysteries are
    a. an ancient, unbroken tradition of Witchcraft
    b. a series of riddles the initiate must answer
    c. an ancient Greek reenactment of the Goddess's descent to and return from the underworld
    d. the secrets found within a coven and passed down by the High Priestess to her initiates

35. Witches believe that after death
    a. we rest in the Summerland
    b. we are reincarnated
    c. we are absorbed into the infinite
    d. there is no universal belief regarding what happens following death

36. In the early 1970s, the British scientist James Lovelock put forth the Gaia hypothesis. What is the Gaia hypothesis?
    a. new archaeological evidence involving the worship of Greek Goddesses
    b. the idea that all living matter on the planet is a part of a single organism
    c. a mixed drink
    d. a Goddess-centric theory on the origins of all life

37. Eco-magic is
    a. based upon the magical principles of recycling
    b. magic involving the use of canyons and reflective sounds
    c. magic based on natural Earth energies and the resident spirits of the land
    d. a made-up term

38. What is the feminine Divine?
    a. the Goddess
    b. the manifestation of feminine energies inherent in the world around us

    c. a performer who appeared in many movies by John
       Waters

    d. a Priestess

39. How many Gods and Goddesses are there?
    a. two
    b. infinite
    c. one
    d. none

40. The following term refers to the psychological and emo-
    tional crossing of a threshold, granting entrance to the oc-
    cult mysteries:
    a. marriage
    b. initiation
    c. elevation
    d. rite of passage

41. What number is most prominent in myth, mysticism, folk
    magic, ritual, and Wicca?
    a. thirteen
    b. two
    c. eleven
    d. three

42. According to Ronald Hutton, a noted religious historian,
    there are "three core beliefs" found in contemporary Pagan-
    ism. They are
    a. love and kinship with Nature; the Wiccan Rede; the Di-
      vine masculine and feminine
    b. a link to the ancient past; polytheism; reincarnation
    c. threefold law of return; reincarnation; working magic
    d. love and kinship with Nature; the Wiccan Rede; the
      threefold law of return

43. In Wicca, what does the term *Third Degree* refer to?
    a. a cold shoulder and silent stare of annoyance from your
      working partner
    b. the third point of a pentacle

   c. a burn that covers more than 40 percent the body or involves blackening of the skin
   d. the highest level of initiation granted in many Wiccan
Traditions

44. What is a Witch Queen?
   a. a flamboyantly gay Witch who typically wears lots of
lavender-colored clothing and rhinestone jewelry, and in-
sists on singing show tunes to invoke the quarters
   b. a Priestess who has had a Priestess leave her coven to start
her own
   c. a Priestess who has obtained the rank of Third Degree
   d. a made-up term without any real use in Wicca

45. An Elder in the Pagan community is seen as
   a. someone who has lived to a ripe old age
   b. someone who has obtained many degrees of initiation
through a number of different Wiccan Traditions
   c. someone who has obtained a high level of respect within
the community for his or her experience, skill, wisdom,
and maturity
   d. someone who has obtained a Third Degree in a Tradition

46. Who are the Ancient Ones?
   a. a rock band from the 1960s
   b. Gerald Gardner, the Farrars, Aleister Crowley, and so
forth
   c. the Gods, the Elements, the Ancestors
   d. anyone over thirty

47. What is PST?
   a. Pacific Standard Time
   b. Psychic Semantics Training
   c. the Pictish Sorcery Tradition
   d. Pagan Standard Time

SECTION 3

Why Do We Do It This Way? Because It's the Tradition!

Some Witches are self-taught. They listen to the wind and to the Earth and let the spirits guide them. The majority of modern Witches, however, are trained in their Craft by another Witch, an individual they respect, or by a group of people within a coven structure. Just as there are hosts of opinions, so there are hundreds of different ways to practice modern Witchcraft.

48. What is a Tradition?
    a. a repeated action
    b. a shared practice or belief handed down through genera-
       tions
    c. anything you don't know the reason for
    d. respect or support

49. What defines a Wiccan or Pagan Tradition?
    a. the length of time it has been practiced
    b. whether or not there has been a book written about it
    c. whether it has an unbroken lineage
    d. spiritual connection with a shared culture, pantheon, or
       magical practice whose form of practice has, or can be,
       transmitted

50. What does it mean when Witches talk about their lineage?
    a. the formal AKC papers they receive upon registering with
       their Tradition
    b. the line of descent from the founder of their Tradition to
       themselves
    c. their hereditary family tree through blood
    d. the immediate members within their coven

51. How many Wiccan Traditions are currently practiced world-
    wide?
    a. unknown
    b. two
    c. seventy-five
    d. 2,384

52. The only way to become a member of this Tradition is to be born into it. This is called a _____Witch:
    a. solitary
    b. lineage
    c. homegrown
    d. hereditary

53. What was the first Wiccan Tradition?
    a. hereditary
    b. Alexandrian
    c. Seax-Wica
    d. Gardnerian

54. This Tradition is a modern reconstruction of the indigenous religion of Northern Europe:
    a. Celtica
    b. Asatru
    c. Minoan
    d. Reclaiming

55. A composite of Gardnerian, Alexandrian, and traditional Wicca plus individual additions, this eclectic Tradition was founded by the late George Patterson:
    a. Dianic
    b. Gardnerian
    c. Georgian
    d. Seax-Wica

56. Alexandrian Wicca was founded by this self-proclaimed "King of the Witches":
    a. Alexei Kondratiev
    b. Samuel Alexander
    c. Lady Bridget and Lord Alcis
    d. Alex Sanders

57. The main difference between Gardnerian and Alexandrian practice is
    a. Gardnerians place more emphasis on the Goddess
    b. the primary forms of the God and Goddess worshiped

    c. Alexandrians place more emphasis on Ceremonial Magic

    d. because Alexandrian originated from Gardnerian, there is very little difference between them

58. Who is credited with having brought the Gardnerian Tradition to the United States?
    a. Raymond Buckland
    b. Doreen Valiente
    c. Gerald Gardner
    d. Leo Martello

59. This term is slang for a Tradition that was inherited, passed down, or learned from your parents or grandparents:
    a. Fam Trad
    b. hereditary
    c. herd
    d. old trad

60. This Tradition has two branches that share the same name and worship the same primary Goddess, yet the sects are radically different in their practices:
    a. Feri
    b. Dianic
    c. Feraferia
    d. Imbas

61. Combining Celtic myth with Huna Traditions of the Hawaiian Islands, this Tradition works with the sensual elements of the senses and ecstatic states:
    a. Dianic
    b. Roebuck
    c. AphroPan
    d. Feri

62. This is a predominantly gay male movement. Its members are noted for their unusual ritual attire, unorthodox practices and strong political leanings:
    a. the Radical Faeries

  b. the Minoan Brotherhood

  c. the Bacchus Brothers

  d. the Gay Blades

63. Originally trained in the Gardnerian Tradition, he broke away to create his own Tradition based on Saxon Traditions and known as Seax-Wica:

  a. Leo Martello

  b. Mark Roberts

  c. Raymond Buckland

  d. Robert Cochrane

64. This Neo-Pagan religous movement was inspired by the book *The White Goddess* and the novel *Watch the North Wind:*

  a. Blue Star

  b. Feraferia

  c. Minoan

  d. Protean

65. Which of the following would be an example of reconstructionism?

  a. Nova Roma

  b. Imbas

  c. Asatru

  d. all of the above

66. What are the primary differences between Ceremonial Magic and Wiccan practices?

  a. Wicca is more formal and organized in its practice

  b. Ceremonial Magic focuses heavily upon theology and form

  c. Ceremonial Magic uses an elaborate system of symbolism, numbers, colors, and timing

  d. Wicca has an unbroken line reaching back to prehistoric times, while Ceremonial Magic dates as far as the Middle Ages

67. This Tradition arose from a work collective that started by

offering classes in Goddess spirituality. It's run by consensus; members are often both spiritually and politically active:
a. Mixed-Gender Dianic
b. Feri
c. Reclaiming
d. Protean

68. The Feri tradition was cofounded by:
a. Victor and Cora Anderson
b. Victor Anderson and Gwydion Pendderwen
c. Victor Anderson and Starhawk
d. Victor Anderson and Morgan McFarland

69. This Tradition was founded in the 1970s in Pennsylvania. Its growth can be attributed to two popular Pagan musicians who, in their travels, established study groups across the country:
a. Protean
b. Minoan
c. Blue Star
d. "1734"

70. The founders of this Tradition were all trained Witches who wanted a Tradition that celebrated gay and lesbian spirituality. It is split into three branches, a men's, women's, and combined groups:
a. Roebuck
b. Minoan
c. Feri
d. Threefold

71. Dianic Wicca was cofounded in the 1960s by:
a. Morgan McFarland and Mark Roberts
b. Z. Budapest and Starhawk
c. Mary Condren and Frederick McLaren Adams
d. Sylvia Eisler and Robert Cochrane

72. This group is dedicated to the rediscovery and revival of the ancient Pagan Celtic mysteries. In 1989, the ancient Keltic

Church was incorporated in the United States and was established as a modern-day Celtic mystery school:
a. Imbas
b. Ár nDraíocht Féin
c. Seax-Wica
d. Roebuck Tradition

73. He was the founder and head magister of the Clan of Tubal
Cain. His death did not cut off his voice—his letters and papers continued his legacy. He described his practice as
hereditary and gave it the name "1734" Tradition:
a. Robert Cochrane
b. Gerald Noel
c. Joe Wilson
d. Anton Wilson

74. These covens or solitaries do not practice a single Tradition
but mix and match from a variety, using whatever appeals to
them at the time:
a. homegrown
b. nontraditional
c. eclectic
d. Shaman-Witch

75. The inspiration for this movement came from a science-
fiction novel, *A Stranger in a Strange Land*, by Robert Hein-
lein. The movement takes the name from the church
founded by the main character in the book, along with the
salutation "Thou art God":
a. the Strange Land Church
b. the Church of All Worlds
c. the Church of Water
d. the Church of Bob

76. Founded in the late 1960s, the name of this Tradition is so
long that it's most often referred to by its initials:
a. the New Reformed Orthodox Order of the Golden Dawn
b. the Sacred Pentacle in Religious Archetypal Learning
c. Witches in Transition Creating Heaven
d. Sacred Initiation in Love, Life and Yearning

SECTION 4
Your Gods Are My Myth

Wicca and Paganism are, in general, polytheistic. We acknowledge a wide variety of Gods, Goddesses, and pantheons. Some of our deities have been actively worshiped on a continuous basis for centuries. Others have been reawakened after years, and sometimes centuries, through reconstructionist religions. Other Gods have been lost to time, with just fragments of their myths or worn depictions carved on stone remaining. We may have little knowledge of their role in the world or how their worship was originally enacted, but the power of these forgotten Gods still echoes over the centuries and is heard by some Witches.

An entire trivia book could be written on the Gods through time. I've narrowed the questions and cultures to the three most frequently recognized in Wiccan circles—Celtic, Norse, and Greek/Roman. You'll probably recognize a few old friends, and maybe be introduced to a few new. If you find something, or someone, that interests you, go to your local bookstore and locate a couple of books on the mythology of that culture. Make sure you do research before inviting a deity into your home. You may find that He or She is like an awful houseguest and is difficult to remove after having settled in!

Celtic/Anglo-Saxon

77. The Mabinogion is
    a. a collection of Welsh stories from the Middle Ages, many reflecting on earlier Celtic Traditions
    b. a Celtic Goddess of war
    c. a Celtic reenactment myth, similar to the Eleusinian mysteries
    d. a Welsh epic poem that provides insights into Celtic religious beliefs and practices

78. Her name means "panic," and as an aspect of Morrigan and

the Consort of the war God Neit, She flies over the battle-fields as a raven or crow inspiring fear and blood lust:

a. Mula
b. Nemain
c. Paneu
d. Orcus

79. Which Celtic Goddess was the only one to have been worshiped in Rome itself and whose worship was spread through the regions of Roman occupation?

a. Bridget
b. Ostara
c. Epona
d. Nemesis

80. This Celtic deity is known by name only from a single Gaulish altar inscription, yet He is popular within many Wiccan circles:

a. Dagda
b. Cernunnos
c. Herne
d. Gobniu

81. This is one of the oldest Celtic pastoral deities of solar worship and healing:

a. Boann
b. Amaethon
c. Belenus
d. Don

82. She prepared the cauldron of knowledge from which the poet Taliesin inadvertently drank:

a. Cathubodua
b. Condatis
c. Coventina
d. Ceridwen

83. Often His image is found in medieval churches; He has also become associated with May Day and fertility:

    a. Jack-in-the-Green
    b. Lenus
    c. John Barleycorn
    d. Pwyll

84. You will find images of Sheela na Gig carved above the doorways of English and Irish churches. Placed there centuries ago by the builders, Her image is considered obscene by the church. Why?
    a. She is a remnant and reminder of the Old faith
    b. She is exposing and cradling Her full breasts
    c. She is exposing Her vagina
    d. She is squatting and giving birth

Norse

85. These three are called the Norns. In Old Norse, they are the triple aspects who control fate and make Their home between the roots of the World Tree:
    a. Klotho, Lachesis, Atropos
    b. Disir, Gefjon, Rind
    c. Enie, Menie, Minnie
    d. Urdr, Verdandi, Skuld

86. Yggdrasil is
    a. a creature of the underworld in Norse mythology
    b. the horse ridden by Odin
    c. the World Tree in Norse mythology
    d. the sword of Odin in Norse mythology

87. Which Goddess invented the Nordic sport of skiing from the ruins of Her marriage bed?
    a. Sigyn
    b. Skadi
    c. Ran
    d. Frigg

88. He hung upon the World Tree to gain knowledge:

    a. Odin
    b. Balder
    c. Thor
    d. Loki

89. How did Odin lose His eye?
    a. in a battle against the Frost Giants
    b. given freely in exchange for wisdom
    c. He was accidentally shot with an arrow by Baal
    d. in a marital spat with Frigg, who punctured it with a knife

90. Of the nine worlds in Norse mythology, the Gods live in Asgard. Where is Freya's home?
    a. Vanaheim
    b. Asgard
    c. Midgard
    d. Svartalfheim

91. If you want to make a reciprocal oath with one of the Norse Gods, with which one would you enjoy the best chance of having the promise fulfilled?
    a. Odin
    b. Thor
    c. Loki
    d. none of the above—none of the Norse Gods can be trusted!

92. Odin rides an unusual eight-legged, winged horse. What is his name?
    a. Sleipnir
    b. Ragnarok
    c. Valknut
    d. Berserks

Greek/Roman

93. This Goddess loaned Her name to a line of sneakers:
    a. Logos

    b. Bia

    c. Klotho

    d. Nike

94. This God isn't wearing sneakers, but He is known for being fleet of foot:

    a. Boreas

    b. Mercury

    c. Zeus

    d. Pan

95. This item caused quite an uproar when it was rolled between three Goddesses, eventually leading to the Trojan War. What was it?

    a. a pomegranate

    b. a golden apple

    c. a beautiful youth contained in a carpet

    d. a silver ball

96. This Goddess of the moon rides a chariot pulled by shining, winged white horses:

    a. Diana

    b. Hecate

    c. Selene

    d. Artemis

97. Integrated into culture, His five-day festival is still joyously celebrated today:

    a. Posis Das

    b. Helios

    c. Plutos

    d. Saturnus

98. The personification of undisciplined nature and wild procreation, He had a bad habit of chasing after young women and frightening travelers:

    a. Pan

    b. Bacchus

    c. Hermes

    d. Adonis

99. Hecate, the patroness of the Witches, has become a popular deity among many Wiccan and Pagan Traditions. She was worshiped in antiquity as_____. She is often depicted_____. One of Her symbols is/are_____.
    a. a goddess of the full moon; without a face; a sickle
    b. a Maiden; carrying a torch; keys
    c. a huntress; with a bow; a willow tree
    d. a man; with a knife; a dog

100. This God of the void loaned His name to both a magical and a modern scientific theory:
    a. Gaia
    b. Hercules
    c. Chaos
    d. Kronos

Who's Your Mama?

101. They gave birth to the Gods, Goddesses, and often the world itself! Match up each Mother Goddess with Her culture of origin (1 point for each correct answer):

1. Inanna _____	A. Egyptian
2. Ishtar _____	B. Aztec
3. Demeter _____	C. Greek
4. Isis _____	D. Celtic—Welsh
5. Astarte _____	E. Kaffir (Afghanistan)
6. Frigg _____	F. Roman
7. Asherat _____	G. Mesopotamian— Babylonian
8. Danu _____	H. Hindu
9. Coatlicue _____	I. Yoruba (West Africa)
10. Don _____	J. Mesopotamian— Sumerian
11. Matres _____	K. Canaanite
12. Parvati _____	L. Celtic—Irish
13. Ceres _____	M. Phoenician

14. Disani   _____   N. Roman/Celtic
15. Papatuanuku _____   O. Norse—Icelandic
16. Oya   P. Polynesian

The Not-Quite-Dead-Yet Gods

102. They gave their lives for the cause. Match up each dying, dead, and reborn God with His culture of origin (1 point for each correct answer):

1. Osiris   _____ A. Mesopotamian
2. Adonis   _____ B. Celtic
3. Attis   _____ C. Celtic—Irish
4. Maponos   _____ D. Polynesian—Maori
5. Balder   _____ E. Christian
6. Milomaki   _____ F. Makoni (East Africa)
7. Quetzalcoatl   _____ G. Egyptian
8. Miach   _____ H. Roman
9. Nommo   _____ I. Syrian/Greek
10. Dumuzi/Tammuz _____ J. Norse
11. Mwuetsi   _____ K. Yahunga/Tukano (upper Amazon)
12. Jesus   _____ L. Dogon (West Africa)
13. Pluto   _____ M. Phrygian
14. Tan (Mahuta)   _____ N. Toltec/Aztec

Answers to Chapter 1

Unless otherwise stated, give yourself *2 points for each correct answer.* Total your points at the end of each section. These totals will be added together at the end of the chapter, giving you a final score for the chapter. This final score will be carried forward to the end of the book for your final count and I.Q. evaluation!

SECTION 1
Wicca and Witches

1. A. Wicca is a contemporary Earth-based religion that acknowledges the sacred found within Nature and honors the Divine in the forms of both a God and Goddess. It is also called modern Witchcraft.

2. C. The Craft or The Craft of the Wise. You might be familiar with this term from a horror movie produced in the 1990s titled *The Craft.*

3. A. *Wiccan* is the adjectival form of *Wicca.* Some Witches prefer the term *Wiccan,* because it does not have the same negative connotations as the word *Witch.* Did you pick B? A Witch is a magic worker. Witches can be found within all cultures and faiths. Not all Witches consider themselves members of the Wiccan religion, although the vast majority of Wiccans do call themselves Witches.

4. B. While witchcraft has been practiced throughout the world for centuries, it is only a romantic notion that the religion of Wicca has an unbroken line to the ancient past. There is no evidence that any organized religion of witch-

craft beyond folk traditions or Ceremonial Magic existed before Gerald Gardner.

5. C. The Old English word for "witch"—*wicce* for the feminine and *wicca* for the masculine—seems to have provided the basis for the modern word *Wicca*.

6. A. The word means "country dweller" or "one who does not live in a city." Cities, of course, are where the smart, trendy, and refined folk live . . . those sensible people who have grown up and rejected silly ideas such as "spirits found in nature." In other words—a Pagan is a country hick! Later, the word came to be associated with those who did not practice Christian beliefs.

7. D. All of these words could fit as a description, but the question asked for an *adaptation* of the word *Pagan*. The prefix *neo* recognizes the difference in practices between the Pagan rites of our ancient ancestors and those of contemporary Paganism. We only know some of the rituals our ancestors performed, and some of them are no longer socially acceptable (it is so hard to find a good bull at a reasonable price for sacrifice nowadays, and the offering of children or slaves just isn't as welcome as it used to be). Neo-Paganism acknowledges that our rites have changed and evolved over time, along with our culture. Neo-Paganism encompasses modern Witchcraft or Wicca and other Pagan religions such as Druidry and Asatru.

8. C. Although individual groups and traditions may be extremely organized and, in some cases, have a hierarchical structure, in general we're an independent lot who hate to be told what to do, believe, or not believe.

9. A. The movement of energy is magic, but when Witches cast a spell they are manipulating the magical forces within themselves and in Nature and focusing them toward a specific goal. They are facilitating change, altering consciousness or physical reality in accordance with their desires, or

will. Among Witches, the belief in magic is universal, along with the sense that there are those who know how to control it.

10. D. Our ancestors who practiced the arts of magic would have fallen into two categories. The first is the village healers, the herbalists, the cunning men or women who provided spells to find lost articles or alleviate ailments that might have been brought about by Witchcraft. The second are the Ceremonial Magicians. They were found among the educated and upper class. Their complicated ritual forms would not have been practiced, or understood, by the lower class, who were often illiterate. Modern Witchcraft, as practiced today, is a unique combination of folk traditions, fragments of Pagan celebrations, Ceremonial Magic, and other occult bits.

11. B. While most Witches do consider themselves to be Pagan, being a Witch and practicing Wicca is only one of the many forms of Paganism. Not all Pagan Traditions practice magic or consider themselves Witches.

12. A. Witches work with the energies, their own and those found in Nature around them, to help create balance and facilitate change. While many Witches are competent in some form of divination, the art of future seeing, others have trouble finding where they left their socks! If you picked C, although some covens do practice skyclad, you have seen far too many horror films in which the director has projected his or her own fantasies into the story. If you thought D, you need to know that a Witch does not work manipulative magic, the forcing of another's will to do the Witch's bidding. It is considered very unethical and plain bad manners.

13. C. An argument might be made for B—but not all Witches work within a coven or community.

14. B. Arguably, just as red hair is passed down genetically, there are families who seem to have inherent psychic talents.

Still, everybody has some level of psychic ability. Just like a muscle, it needs to be stretched and developed in order for it to work efficiently. A competent Witch has taken the time to learn how to strengthen and direct these natural abilities to work magic. It should be noted that while most Wiccans practice magic, not all do.

15. C. What makes a Witch is a personal connection with the God and Goddess and a commitment to practice the beliefs and ethics of Wicca. You may be born into a Witch family (also called hereditary), but not believe or practice the faith. Most people who have become Wiccan were not born into the religion but have left their churches and faiths of origin to practice a new religion. I know Witches who collect initiations the way Boy Scouts collect badges! You can be initiated into a Wiccan tradition, but if you have no emotional or spiritual connection, then you're just going through the motions. And you can receive a prophetic dream or vision but reject it.

16. D. Only you and the Gods know when you have become a Witch. Most initiations, whether with a Tradition, eclectic, or solitary, include a promise made by the Dedicant to the Gods. Whether it was heard and accepted can only be seen within your heart.

TOTAL YOUR POINTS
Chapter 1, Section 1: Wicca and Witches

_____ Total number of questions 1–16 answered correctly

Multiply your total number of questions 1–16 answered correctly by 2. This will give you your total number of points for chapter 1, section 1:

_____16_____ X 2 = _____32_____
Total number of questions   Total score, chapter 1,
1–16 answered correctly   section 1

(For example: 10 correct. 10 x 2 = a total of 20 points for chapter 1, section 1.)

Total possible points for chapter 1, section 1 = 32

SECTION 2

Walking the Walk and Talking the Talk—
Beliefs and Vocabulary

17. C. In general, whether male or female, a Witch is a Witch. Warlocks are Witches gone astray, breaking their oaths or violating ethical conduct by performing baneful magic. The title *Magus* is found in Ceremonial Magic, bestowed on one highly adept at the art. A consort is a partner, wife, husband, or lover. The Horned God is the Consort of the Goddess. However, some of this is also tradition-specific. In some traditions, the title *Magus* is given to the consort, the High Priest, of a Witch Queen.

18. A. A coven. It comes from the Latin word *convenire,* meaning "to come together." It is also where we get the word *convent.*

19. B. *Immanence,* as a religious term, is the concept that the Divine is found within everything—Nature, buildings, ourselves, and each other; we are not separate from the Divine. This is one of the primary beliefs within the Wiccan faith. This contrasts with Judeo-Christian beliefs that hold deity as transcendent. In Christian mythology, God the Father is an example of complete transcendence in that He created everything but exists separate from His creation. There is often a misunderstanding that *eminent* means "transcendence." The dictionary indicates that *eminent* means "prominent" and "famous." I suppose it may appear that famous people are transcendent from the average population, but the intent isn't the same in religious terms.

20. A. Wiccans believe that the Gods are within all of Nature,

the universe, and each other. The world is alive and sacred because it is all Divine!

21. B.   This might sound a bit like pantheism, but it takes the concept one step farther. Animism is the belief that not only are the Gods within everything, but there is also a spiritual consciousness within everything. An animal has a soul, just as a tree also has a sense of existence. Eating dinner and giving thanks for the meal takes on a whole new meaning when you look at life this way.

22. D.   Henotheism is the concept that although you may focus your worship on one deity, the others don't disappear or not exist. The worshiping of one doesn't nullify the existence of the others. You can worship Aphrodite and have your Isis, too!

23. B.   Hermetics is based largely on the works accredited to Hermes Trismegistus, a mythical alchemist who was said to be the grandson of Adam and a builder of the Egyptian pyramids. The works consisted of forty-two sacred books, most of which have been lost, which contained the philosophy of the Egyptians, Priestly training, and teachings on the energies of elements, polarity, and self-transformation. Much of modern magical practice, its symbolism, and spells and rituals in contemporary Wicca and other occult traditions were influenced by Hermeticism.

24. A.   Wicca is, in general, a polytheistic religion, meaning that it recognizes the existence of multiple Gods and Goddesses. Some Witches are monotheistic in that they believe that the Gods and Goddesses are all parts of one great deity. This All is worshiped in both the masculine and feminine forms, as a reflection of Nature. Some Wiccans are dualistic. This is the belief that all Gods are one God and all Goddesses are one Goddess. Still others view each of the Gods and Goddesses as a very real, individual deity. If anything, Wicca is diverse!

25. C.   Akasha makes up the fifth point on the Pentacle, the

spirit or center from which all the elements are joined. Borrowed from Hinduism, it refers to a dimension of space related by vibration or sound.

26. A. Carl Jung saw archetypes as symbols of the subconscious formulated through the collective unconscious. He noted that there were similarities throughout the various cultures of the world within their myth structures—the concept of the Mother Goddess, for example. To some who practice Wicca, these archetypal energies form the basis of the various Gods and Goddesses.

27. D. *Egregore,* "having a group mind," is vital in coven work. It means sharing the same vocabulary, the same goals, ethics, beliefs. In working magic with a group, everyone needs to be "on the same page," focusing on the same goal and vision, in order for the spell to work to its best capacity. For example, visualize an apple. Now, you might be seeing in your mind a red McIntosh apple, while I'm focusing on a green Granny Smith. When there is egregore, we would both call to mind the same variety of fruit!

28. B. Elementals, also called Nature spirits, embody the four elements. They are: earth (gnomes), air (sylphs), fire (salamanders), and water (undines). They can be called upon to assist in magical workings.

29. C. Some Witches prefer to follow their own visions and not work with a coven. They are said to be working solitary. These Witches may or may not be practicing a particular Wiccan tradition. This is not to say they are antisocial! You'll find many solitaries kicking up their heels at community events with other members of the Pagan and Wiccan community. It is in their daily religious practice that they "vant to vorship alone."

30. A. Wicca is not a religion "of the book." It is based on personal experience and connection with the Divine. We do not have a "bible," although the texts named are held in high regard by many Witches.

31. C. The complete phrase is: "Eight words the Wiccan Rede fulfill, an it harm none, do what ye will." The exact origin is uncertain. Gwen Thompson first published the Wiccan Rede in the 1970s in *Green Egg*, a Pagan magazine. It has been thought to have been adapted from Aleister Crowley's Law of Thelema, which is answer B. Others believe that Crowley copied it from an earlier source. It's a mystery and a point of debate taken up during many a late-night gathering of Witches.

32. D. The threefold law of return is based on the concept of cause and effect. Simply put, whatever energy you send out, whether for good or for ill, will return to you three times. It is considered a major deterrent for working manipulative magic and an incentive for working good energy.

33. C. The most familiar form of the Charge of the Goddess was written by Doreen Valiente when she was a member of Gerald Gardner's coven in England. She contributed some of the most beautiful rites and inspirational poetry known in the modern Craft. Of all of them, the Charge has been the most famous.

34. C. In the Eleusinian mysteries of death and rebirth, the maiden Kore is stolen by Hades and brought to the underworld. When Her mother, Demeter, Goddess of agriculture and growth, finds out what happened to Her, She goes into mourning and stops producing the crops. With the help of Hecate, Demeter manages to regain Her daughter but, because Kore ate six seeds from a pomegranate, She is required to return to the underworld for six months out of every year. From this we get the seasons and cycles of life. In spring, the world explodes with Demeter's joy. In summer, She is content. In fall, Her daughter leaves and the world cries; and in winter, Demeter mourns again. The reenactment of the descent and return is a central piece within many mystery traditions.

35. D. Although most Witches do believe in some form of rein-

carnation, there is no dogma or required belief among Wiccans as to what happens following death.

36. B. Doesn't this theory sound familiar? It is something that we Witches and Pagans have known for a long time. The Earth and all things can be understood as interconnected like a gigantic web. Touch one strand and it sends out ripples that affect the other threads. With the Gaia hypothesis, the scientific community finally caught up with us!

37. C. While many Witches, in their awareness of the planet and our interconnection to it, choose to recycle their garbage, this is not the basis of eco-magic. The term instead refers to the awareness of and working with the spirits of the land on which you live (as compared to those in China, Eastern Europe, or even in the town next door from you).

38. B. The feminine Divine is manifestation of the feminine energies, of which the Goddess is one form.

39. A, B, C, and D are all correct, because this is purely a matter of personal opinion. Some people believe that all the Gods and Goddesses are part of the All, the One. Others view the creative powers as dualistic, all Gods are one God and all Goddesses are one Goddess. Others believe that the deities are all different, unique, and immeasurable. And then there are the atheist Witches who work with natural energies but do not believe in the Gods' existence at all! Who's to say who's right? Give yourself the points for answering!

40. B. Initiation is the entrance to the mysteries. Wicca is a mystery religion. Initiation brings the Dedicant to the spiritual doorway, the passage through which marks becoming a member of the tradition and the coven and allows the Dedicant to begin learning the Tradition's ritual secrets and practices.

41. D. The number three has played a major role in many religions. There is the Maiden-Mother-Crone and the threefold law in Wicca. The Third Degree is the highest level of initi-

ation in many Wiccan traditions. Then there is the Father-Son-Holy Spirit in Christianity and Brahma-Shiva-Vishnu in Hinduism; the three pillars in the Kabbalah of Jewish mysticism; in Zen Buddhism, past-present-future and the Three Fates. The list could be longer, but I think you get the point—three is an important number!

42. A.   Surprised? According to Hutton, most Pagans believe in the "threefold law" but not all. Many work magic, but not all. Most believe in some form of reincarnation but again, not everyone. The only three things that seem to be agreed on by Pagans are listed in A.

43. D.   In many traditions, a Third Degree in the highest level of initiation to be completed. It allows Witches to hive off their initial coven to form their own and to initiate other Witches into their tradition.

44. B.   A Witch Queen is a Priestess who has had a Priestess fully trained in her Tradition leave and start her own coven in that Tradition. This act is also referred to as having hived. The exact number of hived Priestesses required for the title of *Witch Queen* is tradition-specific, usually ranging from one to three.

45. C.   Various Traditions will recognize a Third Degree in their sect as an Elder of that tradition. In the Pagan community, however, age and number of initiations or degrees has no actual bearing on who is considered an Elder. The label *Elder* is rarely used by those who are viewed as such. It is earned through the respect of those within their community. These are the people who are often called upon for advice in difficult situations involving the community and are often found working unselfishly for the betterment of the community—not for the stroking of their own egos.

46. C.   The spirits, those who are ageless and can be called upon to help with magical workings.

47. A. This was a trick question. Most Pagans think of *PST* as "Pagan Standard Time," which seems to fall somewhere between half an hour and an hour behind standard time, but *PST* is actually "Pacific Standard Time" . . . make sure to set your watches accordingly.

 TOTAL YOUR POINTS
Chapter 1, Section 2: Beliefs and Vocabulary

___3̲1̲___ Total number of questions 17–47 answered correctly

Multiply your total number of questions 17–47 answered correctly by 2. This will give you your total number of points for chapter 1, section 2:

___3̲7̲___ X 2 = ___6̲2̲___
Total number of questions   Total score, chapter 1,
17–47 answered correctly   section 2

Total possible points for chapter 1, section 2 = 62

SECTION 3

Why Do We Do It This Way?
Because It's the Tradition!

48. B. A Tradition is like a habit—you just keep doing it and doing it until it's such a part of you that you can't imagine not doing it. There is an Imbolc ritual enacted by the Reclaiming Collective each year in the San Francisco area. As part of the ritual, the adults make a yearly pledge to the Goddess Bridget. The organizers of the rite once thought about changing it until they realized that the next generation—those children who had attended over the years—had reached the age to come forward to state their own yearly vows. These young adults were looking forward with great anticipation to their opportunity to participate in this rite!

They couldn't just stop or change the ritual. It had become a Tradition that was expected to occur, just like decorating a tree at Yule and singing "Happy Birthday" when blowing out the candles on a birthday cake have become Traditions.

49. D. The proof is in the pudding, as they say. Can the practice be passed down (or has it been passed down) and, more important, will it be continued? If yes, then it is a Tradition.

50. B. This is the line of transmission going back to the founder of the tradition. Some people think it's silly to care where your practice came from. Others are overly interested in lineage, even disregarding the initiations of entire lines within their own Tradition if they disagree with the teachings or training of an initiating Priest or Priestess back two generations. There can be an argument for C, because some Traditions are strictly hereditary, but this definition is limiting. Both hereditary Traditions and those passed down through training or initiation fit into B.

51. A. It is unknown how many Wiccan Traditions are currently practiced. All we do know is that Wicca has been growing by leaps and bounds!

52. D. Hereditary Craft is a succession of individuals linked through birth, marriage, or adoption and containing the assumption that birth gives the right of membership.

53. D. Witches and Witchcraft have been around for centuries, but it wasn't until the 1950s that a religion based on Witchcraft was formally created. Named after its founder Gerald Gardner, the Gardnerian Tradition is the base from which many of the other Wiccan Traditions were formed. Beliefs include duality, as expressed in the God and Goddess; the cycles of life; and a personal connection with the Gods. The Wiccan Rede is a guiding principle. Both ritual and magic are important. Gardnerian covens are autonomous and hierarchical in nature with three levels of degrees. Initiated members are considered Priests or Priestesses.

For More Information: Triumph of the Moon by Ronald Hutton (Oxford University Press, 1999).

54. B. Asatru is a reconstructed Pagan Tradition. Asatru was formally organized in 1973 and is recognized as a legitimate religion by the Icelandic government. With no central authority, worshipers form groups, called kindreds, that may or may not associate with other kindreds. They are polytheistic, working with the Norse pantheon. Magic is not a part of practice. Asatru is famous for Blóts—rituals involving lots of food and drink that is ritually passed around the circle to be shared by the participants and offered to the Gods through toasts and libations.

    For More Information: Teutonic Religion by Kveldulf Gundarsson.

55. C. Patterson created the Georgian Wiccan Tradition in Bakersfield, California. From there it spread throughout the United States. While incorporating the more traditional traditions, Georgian also encourages individuals to explore and write their own rituals.

56. D. Alexander Sanders claimed that at age seven, he walked into the kitchen to find his grandmother naked, standing in the center of a circle. Right there and then, it is said, she initiated him. There is some evidence that Alex was actually an initiated Gardnerian, but he took the materials and added his own flair.

    For More Information: The Witches' Bible by Janet and Stewart Farrar (Magical Child Publishing, 1984).

57. C. There are many similarities between the Gardnerian and Alexandrian Traditions, but there are a few differences. One of the primary contrasts is that Alexandrians use more ceremonial aspects in their ritual practices.

58. A. Raymond Buckland, who was initiated by Gerald Gardner in 1963, is credited with bringing the tradition to the shores of the United States.

59. A. A Tradition that is passed down within a family is call hereditary. The slang term is *Fam Trad*, for "Family Tradition."

60. B. The Dianic Tradition has a strong focus on the Goddess Diana and the Divine feminine. It has produced two very distinct branches: Dianic Wicca, and Mixed-Gender Dianic Wicca. The original branch was cofounded by a couple in the 1960s. It allowed both women and men to participate and share in the mysteries. Z. Budapest's Dianic tradition is for women only, to the complete exclusion of men. Both structures are nonhierarchical and consensus-based. There are only two levels of initiation—dedication and High Priest or Priestess.

      For More Information: The Grandmother of Time or *The Holy Book of Women's Mysteries*, both by Z. Budapest (Harper & Row, 1989; Wingbow Press, 1989).

61. D. The Feri or Anderson Faery tradition was founded by Victor Anderson and Gwydion Pendderwen. It's an ecstatic Tradition, with an emphasis on the sensual experience and sexual mysticism. It's also polytheistic, with the Gods recognized as individual entities. The Feri Tradition works with visualizations, energy work, direct communication with the Divine, and a doctrine of the Three Selves. Not a rigid system, here all initiates adapt the Tradition by adding their own interests and strengths. Originally called the Faery Tradition, Victor changed the spelling to Feri in order to differentiate it from other groups calling themselves Fairy (having to do with fairies), some of whom were Pagan and others not. The Feri Tradition has given the world more than its share of Wiccan and Pagan elders and stars, to name just a few: Victor and Cora Anderson, Gwydion Pendderwen, Starhawk (*The Spiral Dance*), Macha NighMare (*The Pagan Book of Living and Dying*), and Francesca De Grandis (*Be a Goddess!*). For more information on the Third Road form of the Feri/Faery Tradition: Francesca De Grandis's Web

site, www.well.com/~zthirdrd/. For more information on
the Reclaiming form of Feri/Faery, www.reclaiming.org.

62. A. The first time I met the Radical Faeries was at a gay
pride march in New York City in the early 1990s. They were
a group of about forty-five men, each wearing a pink tutu or
other flamboyant costume, carrying wands with stars and
streamers, sparkly headbands with antennae, or other such
adornments. A few even had wings strapped to their backs. I
thought, "Who are these guys?" as they flittered up and down
the street immediately ahead of our "very serious" Pagans
and Witches for Gay Pride contingent. As we approached St.
Patrick's Cathedral, without a word the Faeries came together
and formed a weaving line. When we reached the gates of the
church, the line became a spiral dance spinning with energy.
Most of the Pagans, myself included, found ourselves being
pulled into creating a dazzling cone of energy, which was released for peace and tolerance. They do good work. As you
may have gathered from this story, they are a flamboyant
group of men who enjoy working magic along with making
political statements. They have no hierarchy or strict form of
practice. The Radical Faeries are more a movement than a
Tradition, and not all their members are Pagan.

63. C. In 1973, Raymond Buckland broke away from the
Gardnerian Tradition and founded his own Tradition, which
he called Seax-Wica. It is an interesting blend of different
traditions and celebrations. Primary deities are the Norse
Gods Woden and Freya. There is no oath of secrecy binding
members, and the Tradition is open to change and adaptation. Rituals are solar with optional, though encouraged,
moon rites. Covens are autonomous and democratic. There
is no degree system or initiation.

   For More Information: The Tree by Raymond Buckland
(Samuel Weiser, 1974).

64. B. Feraferia was founded by Frederick McLaren Adams
from a vision that was derived from a number of literary

sources. The word *Feraferia*, is derived from a Latin term meaning "wilderness festival." It celebrates the Wilderness Mysteries with a blending of art, ecology, and mythology.

65. D. All of the above. Reconstructionist traditions attempt to reproduce, as best as can be actualized, the rites and practices of ancient Pagan cultures. The Nova Roma is Italian, Imbas focuses on the Celtic traditions, and Asatru re-creates the Norse. Reconstructionism is not restricted to religious systems. The Society for Creative Anachronism (SCA) is a popular Middle Ages/Renaissance re-creation organization. There are many who reenact American Revolutionary and Civil War battles. Pick a time period, you can probably find a group of folks who want to live it for at least a brief period of time (or until they need to use the bathroom or take a shower).

66. C. Ceremonial Magic is a highly structured occult science. It is *not* considered a Wiccan tradition, but many Wiccan Traditions have their roots in the symbolism and rites of Ceremonial Magic. It has a history that stretches into antiquity to the practices of theurgy, which is a system used by Greek Neoplatonists. Ceremonial Magic works with an intricate and complicated system of numbers, colors, and symbol associations, combined with exact timing. The Kabbalah, taken from Jewish mysticism, also plays an major role in this system. In Ceremonial Magic, there is a stronger emphasis on practice than on theology.

67. C. The Reclaiming Tradition is based on the Feri Tradition. It arose from a work collective in the San Francisco Bay Area in the 1980s. Founded by Starhawk and Diane Baker, it began simply with the offering of classes in the San Francisco area and grew to encompass very successful "Witch Camps" offered in the United States, Canada, and Europe. Reclaiming combines self-empowerment with spirituality with political activism. Unlike many Traditions, it has no requirements for initiation, focuses on no specific pantheon, and has no set liturgy.

For More Information: the Reclaiming Web site, www.reclaiming.org.

68. D. Also known as Anderson Faery, this Tradition was co-founded by Victor Anderson and later expanded by Gwydion Pendderwen. Gwydion was known as a Celtic bard for his musical and other artistic talents. His writings and music have continued to touch many long after his tragic death in 1982. Victor Anderson was introduced at a young age to a style of Witchcraft that emphasized harmony with Nature and used music and ecstatic dance in celebrations. Victor Anderson met Gwydion as a young boy. The story goes that Victor broke up a fight between his son and Gwydion. They developed a friendship, and Victor initiated Gwydion into Witchcraft. Together they wrote many of the rituals for the Feri.

69. C. With a base in Alexandrian, the Blue Star Tradition proudly traces its roots all the way back to the very ancient mid-1970s. Blue Star was founded by Frank Duffner, but it was Tzipora Katz and Kenny Klein, two traveling musicians, who took the Tradition out on the road and spread the faith. Today, Blue Star covens stretch across the United States. Theirs is a hierarchical, degree-based mystery religion and oral Tradition. The actual operation of each coven varies greatly.

70. B. The Minoan Tradition consists of the Minoan Brotherhood, the Minoan Sisterhood, and a combined-gender group, the Cult of the Double Axe/Cult of Rhea. Founded by Eddie Buczynski, Carol Bulzone, and Lady Rhea, the Minoan tradition emphasizes creating a safe and sacred place for gay and bisexual work. The Brotherhood and the Cult of the Double Axe/Cult of Rhea have expanded across the United States and into Canada; the Sisterhood has remained centrally located in New York City.

For More Information: The Witchcraft Fact Book by Eddie Buczynski.

71. A. Morgan McFarland and Mark Roberts cofounded the Dianic Tradition in the 1960s. It was later renamed Mixed-Gender Dianic Wicca to differentiate it from the branch that is limited strictly to women.

72. D. The Roebuck Tradition was founded by Ann and David Finnin in 1976. It is based upon the writings of Robert Cochrane and was inspired by the "1734" Tradition, but it has its own distinct flavor. The Roebuck works with a combination of Irish, Welsh, and Gaelic folklore and emphasizes personal spiritual development over magical practice. Covens are organized in a clan structure and are autonomous. There is only one initiation, through which a member is brought into the clan. It also grants ordination under the Ancient Keltic Church.

    For More Information: the Ancient Keltic Church/Clan of Tubal Cain Web site, http://members.aol.com/CTubal Cain.

73. A. The history of the "1734" Tradition is very complicated. It was established by Joe Wilson in the United States through his correspondences with Robert Cochrane. Following Cochrane's untimely death in 1966, members in the United States continued meeting, basing their practices on the knowledge given to Wilson through these letters. These writings included teachings, but did not contain information about the workings of a coven. Consequently, the "1734" covens borrowed from other Traditions, notably Gardnerian, to fill in the gaps. Considered a mystery religion, "1734" is entered into through initiation. The number "1734" is not a date but contains more mystical meaning.

    For More Information: "1734 Tradition" the Ancient Keltic Church/Clan of Tubal Cain Web site at http:// ancientkelticchurch.org.

74. C. An eclectic Witch practices diversity. He or she takes ideas from many different sources and Traditions—from

Gardnerian to Shamanism, from Buddhist to Hindu—to create an interesting and very personal meld. Many of the so-called Traditions started out as eclectic. Through time, they developed into a set format of beliefs and practices that were then passed down, thus forming a new Tradition.

75. B. The Church of All Worlds (CAW) was founded by Oberon Zell (formerly Otter G'Zell) and his wife Morning Glory Zell. It is a pantheistic religion. Its goal is finding and experiencing Divinity and achieving union with all consciousness. There are no set beliefs. Groups are called nests and can be found throughout the United States. CAW filed for incorporation in 1967. With the help of the ACLU, it achieved church status in 1971.

76. A. NROOGD started as a class assignment in the late 1960s. It combines various sources, from *The White Goddess* to Gerald Gardner. NROOGD practice focuses on the working of magic and the existence of deity within all. Mythic reenactments are often performed, and large public seasonal rituals for the Pagan community are traditionally offered. The Tradition values poetry and scholarship in its rituals. There are three levels of initiation—white cord, red cord, and black cord/garter—with lineage tracing back to members of the original coven. There is no central authority. Currently found primarily on the West Coast, members exist all over the country.

For More Information: www.nroogd.org.

 TOTAL YOUR POINTS
Chapter 1, section 3: Traditions

_____ Total number of questions 48–76 answered correctly

Multiply your total number of questions 48–76 answered correctly by 2. This will give you your total number of points for chapter 1, section 3:

_____ X 2 = _____

Total number of questions   Total score, chapter 1,
48–76 answered correctly   section 3

Total possible points for chapter 1, section 3 = 58

SECTION 4
Your Gods Are My Myth

77. A. Dating from the fourteenth century (at its completion), this book consists of Welsh mythology but contains little about the actual religious practices of the Celts. Robert Graves, author of *The White Goddess,* theorized that the name *Mabinogion* translates to "juvenile romances." The proper Welsh name is *Mabinogi.*

78. B. The Morrigan is a multiaspect Goddess. As Queen Mabd She is the Goddess of the land; as Nemain and Badb Catha, She is the Goddess of war and battle.
    For Your Learning Enjoyment: Mula is a minor Hindu Goddess of fortune; Paneu is, for the Kafir of Afghanistan, the collective name for the seven Gods, hunters for the Goddess Disani; Orcus is a Roman underworld God.

79. C. Epona is the horse Goddess. Associated with healing and fertility, especially of the herds, She was the only Celtic Goddess worshiped in Rome. She was very popular with the Roman cavalry regiments. Her festival is on December 18.
    For Your Learning Enjoyment: Bridget is a popular pastoral Celtic deity. She is celebrated at Imbolc, the time of lactation of the ewes. Ostara gave Her name to the Christian holiday of Easter. A sun Goddess, She is associated with spring and renewal. Nemesis is a Roman Goddess of justice and revenge, and is associated with the Furies.

80. B. Cernunnos (Cerne) is a version of Horned God and viewed as one of the consorts of the Goddess in modern

Wicca. A God who acts as an interface between Nature and humans and the crossing of boundaries, He is often depicted with antlers on His head. His likeness appears on the famous Gundestrup Cauldron, where He is shown with a boar (the boar is revered by the Celts).

For Your Learning Enjoyment: Dagda is an Irish God. He is the protector of the people and father to Bridget. Herne, as leader of the Wild Hunt, is associated with the underworld. It is possible that many Witches do call upon Gobniu without realizing it, because His skill is as a smith God who also brews beer—a staple in many a Wiccan circle.

81. C. While scholars disagree, popular belief associates Belenus or Bel with Beltane, a Celtic May celebration and one of the major seasonal celebrations on the Wiccan calendar. During His rite, which was held on May 1, cattle were driven between bonfires for protection against disease. Belenus bears some similarities to the Greek God Apollo.

    For Your Learning Enjoyment: Boann means "She of the white cows." She is a river Goddess, in particular of the River Boyne. Amaethon is a God of agriculture and is associated with plowing and husbandry. If Don makes an offer, you can't refuse . . . She is a Mother Goddess figure and ancestress to the Welsh pantheon. She equates with the Irish Goddess Danu.

82. D. Ceridwen is the Celtic Goddess of death, wisdom, inspiration, divination, magic, and science. Her primary symbol was the cauldron. Given Her association with death and regeneration, She is one of the Goddesses sometimes called upon by Wiccans during the seasonal celebration of Samhain (Halloween).

    For Your Learning Enjoyment: Cathubodua is a Celtic war Goddess. Condatis is a Celtic/British river God. Coventina was a purely local British Goddess associated with waterways.

83. A. Jack-in-the-Green is another name for the Green Man. A traditional May Day figure, He is the spirit of the trees

and green growing life. His face, surrounded by leaves, often appears on cathedrals.

For Your Learning Enjoyment: Lenus is a God of healing. John Barleycorn represents the cycles of the grain. Pwyll is sometimes associated with the underworld and credited with bringing the pig to Wales.

84. C. A Crone figure (Irish/English), She stands naked with a grin upon Her face, Her large breasts sagging, Her legs wide apart, Her hands stretching open Her vulva to reveal the mystery within. Carved above doorways of Irish churches in Ireland and parts of England, and amazingly not destroyed over time, these figures are rare depictions of Irish Celtic deities that have survived into the Christian era. Not much is known about Her, and scholars argue about where She originates. It is thought that She represents the primal Earth Goddess of life and death; She stands graphically reminding worshipers of where life emerges and that all life will return to Her womb.

_____ Total number of correct matches in questions 77—84: Celtic

85. D. Urdr (fate—the past), Verdandi (being—the present), Skuld (necessity—the future).

86. C. An ash, Yggdrasil is the cosmic tree with roots that reach into all worlds and boughs that reach above Asgard.

87. B. The patron Goddess of Scandinavia. Gods of Asgard killed her father, who was a giant. She, being a warrior maiden, showed up at the wall of Asgard and demanded blood money or combat. They agreed to pay Her the price and gave Her a husband. The catch was, She had to choose by looking at their feet. She ended up with Njord, God of sea commerce. They got along all right, but just couldn't manage to live together. Finally, She broke up the marriage bed, made skis out of it, and skied home.

For Your Learning Enjoyment: Sigyn is the consort to Loki. To punish Loki, the God Siofn set a poisonous snake that continually dripped venom upon the captive Loki. Sigyn caught the poison in a bowl, saving Her husband. Ran is the Nordic storm Goddess, the consort of the God Aegir. Regarded as Queen of the Heaven, *Frigg* is a Goddess of midwifery, childbirth, and protection of the home.

88. A.   Othin or Odin, which means "all father," is the principal God of victory in battle and of the dead. Obsessed with the pursuit of knowledge, Othin hung Himself on the World Tree, Yggdrasil, to gain the knowledge of the runes. Credited with being a shape-shifter, He is associated with Shamanism. He often wanders the Earth disguised as a traveler with a cloak covering His missing eye.

      For Your Learning Enjoyment: Killed by a dart made of a sprig of mistletoe, *Balder*, the son of Frigg and Othin, resides in the underworld. Armed with His hammer, *Thor* is the God of war, the sky, storms, and justice. *Loki* was not worshiped like the other Asgard deities but, because He's a notorious troublemaker, just saying His name can invoke chaos.

89. B.   Odin or Othin gave His right eye to the God Mimir as payment for permission to drink from the Well of Knowledge, which rises from a spring beneath the roots of the World Tree.

90. A.   This is a trick question because, in a sense, both A and B are true. As a Vanir, Freya's original home was in Vanaheim. Following the war between Aesir and Vanir She became part of a "prisoner exchange" that moved Her to Asgard, hall of the Aesir. So Asgard is where She currently lives but Vanaheim is Her home. It is said to be a realm of great beauty that contains the place of life-giving water.

      For Your Learning Enjoyment: Midgard is our world, our reality. *Svartalfheim* is the dark reaches of the Earth, inhabited by the dark elves, keepers of the Earth's riches.

91. B. Both Odin and Loki are notorious for lying and ignoring pacts made. On the other hand, Thor is considered reliable and trustworthy.

92. A. Sleipnir was born from a mating between the fire God Loki and a mare that belonged to the Frost Giants.

    For Your Learning Enjoyment: Ragnarok is the final day of reckoning when the battle against the Frost Giants will occur. *Valknut* is Othin's knotted rope, which represents the power to bind or unbind minds of warriors and influence the outcome of battles. Othin was the patron God of a fanatical warrior cult called the *Berserks.*

_____   Total number of correct matches in questions 85–92:
Norse

93. D. Nike, Goddess of victory.

    For Your Learning Enjoyment: Logos is the Goddess of reason. *Bia* is the Goddess of force. I haven't seen Her name on anything yet. *Klotho* is a Goddess of spinning—in other words, clothes.

94. B. Also known by the Greeks as Hermes, Mercury (Mercurius) is the swift-footed messenger. Mercury is portrayed with winged sandals and hat (petasus) and carrying a caduceus, a serpent-entwined wand. God of travelers, His image was erected at crossroads.

    For Your Learning Enjoyment: Boreas doesn't need any shoes, because He is the North Wind itself. With Their tendency to get into trouble with the ladies, both Zeus and Pan probably could use Mercury's winged shoes.

95. B. One day a golden apple was rolled into the room where the Gods lived. On it was the note: "to the fairest." A riot among Aphrodite, Hera, and Athena erupted, because each felt She deserved to claim it. It was finally decided to ask a mortal to choose. They selected Paris, a son of a king. Hera promised Paris that She would make him lord of Asia.

Athena promised to make him victorious in battle. To emphasize Her point, Aphrodite removed Her robe and promised him the most beautiful of mortal women. The poor boy didn't have a chance. He chose the woman, who turned out to be Helen—and the rest is history.

96. C. Selene, a winged, silvery Goddess who presides over the night skies, sister to the sun God Helios, rides in her chariot of white. In Roman culture, She equates with the Goddess Luna.
    For Your Learning Enjoyment: All four of the Goddesses have associations with the moon. *Hecate* (Hekate) is the Goddess of pathways and the crossroads traveled by night. Diana is Roman; Her Greek counterpart is Artemis. She is the huntress, protector of animals, as well as the guardian of virginity.

97. D. Saturnalia is the ancient Roman feast in honor of the God Saturnus. This festival began on December 17 and continued for five days, climaxing at the winter solstice. Many of today's Christmas traditions stem from Saturnalia, including feasting, candles, and gift giving. Candles were exchanged to symbolize the winter's darkness. Saturnus was an agriculture God, concerned with the sowing of seeds.
    For Your Learning Enjoyment: As the sky God, *Posis Das* is the consort of the Earth mother, Gaia. *Helios* looks down from the sky as He drives His chariot of the sun. *Plutos* has nothing to do with the sky or the sun, but is associated with shining things and riches.

98. A. Pan is the Greco-Roman God of the shepherds. With His horns, the feet of a goat, and strong phallic associations, He is believed to be the visual model for the Christian concept of the devil. But this boy just wants to have fun! He is known for his pipe playing and amorous advances, and is often invoked within Pagan and Wiccan rituals, especially during Beltane (May Day) and summer festivals.
    For Your Learning Enjoyment: Bacchus would have been close. This God of wine and intoxication can also cause a

ruckus. Hermes is another who can manage to get Himself into trouble with his sexual prowess, but He usually sticks to the roads well traveled. Adonis found His way to the Greek pantheon as an old Semitic dying and reborn God. He is the God of love, beauty, and rebirth.

99. B. Hecate was originally worshiped as a Maiden, but over time She got older. In modern traditions, She is often depicted as the Crone aspect in the triple Goddess of life, death, and rebirth. Hecate is a Goddess of the paths and crossroads traveled at night. She carries a torch to light the way and is often seen with the keys to the mysteries dangling from Her waistband.

100. C. Chaos is the primordial void that existed before the formation of an orderly cosmos in the universe. He is the offspring of the Titan Kronos. Chaos magic, created in the 1970s, is an explanation of why magic works. The Chaos theory, which was popularized in the movie *Jurassic Park,* is a scientific theory on how the universe was created.

_____ Total number of correct matches in questions 93–100: Greek/Roman

Who's Your Mama?

101. Mix and match the mothers (1 point per correct match):

1. Inanna	J	Mesopotamian—Sumerian
2. Ishtar	G	Mesopotamian—Babylonian
3. Demeter	C	Greek
4. Isis	A	Egyptian
5. Astarte	M	Phoenician
6. Frigg	O	Norse
7. Asherat	K	Canaanite
8. Danu	L	Celtic—Irish

9. Coatlicue	_B_ Aztec
10. Don	_D_ Celtic—Welsh
11. Matres	_N_ Roman/Celtic
12. Parvati	_H_ Hindu
13. Ceres	_F_ Roman
14. Disani	_E_ Kaffir (Afghanistan)
15. Papatuanuku	_P_ Polynesian
16. Oya	_I_ Yoruba (West Africa)

1. *Inanna* (Mesopotamian—Sumerian). Queen of Heaven, Goddess of fertility and war. In Her myth, when Her beloved husband Dumuzi dies, She descends to the underworld to challenge Her sister Ereskigal, the Goddess of death. She is stopped and challenged seven times, stripped and bound, and left for dead for three days. Inanna is released at the request of Enki, the God of wisdom. With similarities to the Demeter/Persephone myth, Inanna's husband is allowed to return to the land of the living but only for half of each year. Her rites involved reenactment of the sacred marriage by the king and the High Priestess of Inanna.

2. *Ishtar* (Mesopotamian—Babylonian). Goddess of fertility and war, counterpart to the Sumerian Inanna. Often depicted with weapons. The Egyptians revered her as a Goddess of healing.

3. *Demeter* (Greek). The Mother Goddess associated with vegetation, agriculture, and death; mother of Persephone/Kore. The cult of Demeter was practiced widely and is the heart of the Eleusinian mysteries of death and rebirth. Romans identified Her with Ceres, their Goddess of the Earth.

4. *Isis* (Egyptian). Isis' influence stretched far beyond the edges of the Nile. She was beloved in Rome, and temples dedicated to Isis could be found in Europe. Isis is the mother of the Gods of Egypt and both sister and consort to Osiris, ruler of the under-

world. She and Her son Horus are said to have influenced the portrayal of the Christian Virgin Mary and baby Jesus.

5. *Astarte* (Phoenician/Syrian). Goddess of the evening star, war, and sexual love. In Hellenic times, She became linked with Aphrodite.

6. *Frigg* (Norse/Icelandic). Queen of the Goddesses at Asgard, closely associated with childbirth, midwifery, and protection of the home.

7. *Asherat* (Canaanite). Great Mother Goddess of Canaan. Known as "Lady Asherat of the sea," creatress of the Gods. Her groves are those referred to in the Bible. Very popular religion among the Israelites, to the annoyance of the prophets.

8 *Danu* (Celtic—Irish). She is a Mother Goddess of the Irish pantheon, the Tuatha de Dannann.

9. *Coatlicue* (Aztec). Mother Goddess of Earth and humankind. As the mother of the sun, She plays a major role in the battle between night and day.

10. *Don* (Celtic—Welsh). Described in the Mabinogion as the progenitress of the Welsh pantheon, She equates with the Irish goddess Danu.

11. *Matres* (Roman/Celtic). These are triads of Mother Goddesses. They are often depicted with baskets of fruit, loaves, sheaves of grain, fish, or other symbols of prosperity and fertility.

12. *Parvati* (Hindu). Consort of the God Shiva, She personifies the faithful wife. Mother of Ganesha.

13. *Ceres* (Roman). Modeled after Demeter; daughter of Kronos and Rhea, consort to Jupiter. Her daughter, Kore/ Proserpine, is taken by Pluto, God of the underworld, where She is forced to remain (or willingly stays) for half the year.

14. *Disani* (Kaffir—Afghanistan). Goddess of fertility and death, She guides the dead back home. She also receives the prayers from women for those men who are about to go to battle. Protectress of the family and kin, She is depicted with a bow and quiver, with streams of milk pouring from Her breasts.

15. *Papatuanuku* (Polynesian/Maori). She evolved spontaneously in the womb of night and became the Earth when She was born.

16. *Oya* (Yoruba—West Africa). Companion of the lightning God Shango, She is a fierce Goddess with power over wind, fire, and the spirits of the dead.

_____ Total number of correct matches in question 101: the Goddesses

The Not-Quite-Dead-Yet Gods

102. Mix and match the dying, dead, and reborn Gods (1 point per correct match):

1. Osiris	G	Egyptian
2. Adonis	I	Syrian/Greek
3. Attis	M	Phrygian
4. Maponos	B	Celtic
5. Balder	J	Norse
6. Milomaki	K	Yahunga/Tukano (upper Amazon)
7. Quetzalcoatl	N	Toltec/Aztec
8. Miach	C	Celtic—Irish
9. Nommo	L	Dogon (West Africa)
10. Dumuzi/Tammuz	A	Mesopotamian
11. Mwuetsi	F	Makoni (East Africa)
12. Jesus	E	Christian
13. Pluto	H	Roman
14. Tan (Mahuta)	D	Polynesian (Maori)

1. *Osiris* (Egyptian). Brother-husband of Isis, He is killed and dismembered by His brother Set, but Isis reassembles Him and brings Him back to life.

2. *Adonis* (Syrian/Greek). A God of seasonal cycles, He is the consort of Astarte but is killed by a boar; mourned passionately at His death, He is reborn in the time of spring growth. Hellenistic Greeks adopted the myth, making Aphrodite His consort.

3. *Attis* (Phrygian). Beloved of the Goddess Cybele, He was driven mad by Her when He courted another woman. He castrated himself under a pine tree, but His body was transformed into the undying certainty of the return of spring.

4. *Maponos* (Celtic). Portrayed as a young hunter, He is the beloved of the Goddess during the bright season but is killed by a boar at the coming of winter, only to be reborn in the next cycle. The tale of the hero Diarmuid in the Irish stories about Fionn MacCumhaill and his men is one way this pattern was expressed in Celtic Tradition.

5. *Balder* (Norse). A God of solar beauty and well-being, He was killed with a sprig of mistletoe by His blind brother Hoder. In the Eddas, it is said that He will not return from Hel until after the end of this world, but in earlier times His death and resurrection were probably a seasonal phenomenon.

6. *Milomaki* (Yahunga/Tukano—upper Amazon). A beautiful boy who comes from the house of the sun and entrances everyone with His otherworldly singing, he is nevertheless burned to death when it is discovered that those who listen to His singing die of poisoning as soon as they eat wild foods. From His ashes grows the first paxiuba tree, from which flutes are made that reproduce his singing; when the flutes are sounded, wild foods become edible to humans.

7. *Quetzalcoatl* (Toltec/Aztec). Driven from power by His rival, the God Tezcatlipoca, He immolates himself and His

heart becomes the planet Venus; but He promises to return to the mortal world in a distant future.

8. *Miach* (Celtic—Irish). Son of Dian Cécht, the God of healing, and twin brother to Airmheith (or Airmid), Miach is a miraculous healer who is killed by His father, jealous of His gifts. From His body grow the healing herbs that can cure all the ills of the body. Airmheith classifies all the herbs according to their properties, but Dian Cécht mixes them up again, so herbalism must now be learned through trial and error.

9. *Nommo* (Dogon—West Africa). One of the many children of Amma, the creator Goddess, He is killed and dismembered by Her to make the universe, then brought back to life to rule over the world.

10. *Dumuzi/Tammuz* (Mesopotamian). The consort of Inanna/Ishtar, in some versions of the story His death is the cause of Her descent to the underworld. He symbolizes the vegetation cycle in nature.

11. *Mwuetsi* (Makoni—East Africa). The first God to dwell on the Earth, He also accidentally introduces death into the world. Learning that life for humans will be possible only if He submits to death Himself, He consents to die, but rises again as the Moon.

12. *Jesus* (Christian). Manifesting the creator deity in a perfect human form, He is made to die on a cross bearing the burden of all human suffering, and is resurrected three days later.

13. *Pluto* (Roman). God of the underworld, His Greek counterpart is Hades. He kidnaps the daughter of Ceres, Persephone. He is forced to return Her but not before making a deal that She will return to Him for half of every year.

14. *Tan* (Mahuta) (Polynesian—Maori). God of the forests and consort to Hine-Nui-Te-Po, Goddess of death. Each night

He descends to the underworld to be with Her and returns to life each day.

_____ Total number of correct matches in question 102: The Gods

TOTALING YOUR POINTS
Chapter 1, Section 4: Mythology

Add together your total number of correct matches from the Celtic, Norse, and Greek/Roman sections:

_____ Total number of correct Celtic mythology matches
+ _____ Total number of correct of Norse mythology matches
+ _____ Total number of correct of Greek/Roman mythology matches
= _____ Total Celtic, Norse, and Greek/Roman

Multiply your mythology total by 2, to get your grand total for the 2-point questions:

_____ X 2 = _____
Total number of myth 2-point   Total score, 2-point ques-
questions answered correctly   tions, chapter 1, section 4

Add together your total number of 1-point correct matches from the Goddess and God sections:

_____ Total number of 1-point matches, question 101, the Goddesses
+ _____ Total number of 1-point matches, question 102, the Gods
= _____ Total combined total of 1-point matches, questions 101 and 102

Now add together your 2-point total with your total for the 1-point questions:

_____   +   _____   =   _____

| 2-point questions total | 1-point questions total | Total score, chapter 1, section 4 |

Total possible points for chapter 1, section 4 = 78

TOTALING CHAPTER 1

Add together your totals from each section in chapter 1:

_____ Chapter 1, section 1—Wicca and Witches
+ _____ Chapter 1, section 2—Beliefs and Vocabulary
+ _____ Chapter 1, section 3—Traditions
+ _____ Chapter 1, section 4—Mythology

= [   ] Grand total score for chapter 1

This is the number you will carry forward to the end of the book!

Total possible points for chapter 1 = 230

Tools of the Trade

Within, Without, and All About the Circle

How we Witches love our tools! A tool is something that aids Witches in their practice. It may be physical, such as a wand or a prop that acts as a magical focus; or a tool can be found only in the mind, such as visualization techniques. The circle is a tool for the focusing and directing of energies. A seasonal celebration or festival can also act as a tool. It is a point on the seasonal wheel of life that aids in attuning the practitioners to the cycles of Nature.

SECTION 1

Tools and Toys

1. This is your focal point, where everything for the rite is placed and used during the ritual. It is where devotional items are kept. In effect, it is your own personal microcosm of the universe:
   a. the closet
   b. the library
   c. the altar
   d. the bathroom

2. An altar is traditionally set up in the

   a. center of the circle
   b. northern section of the circle
   c. eastern section of the circle
   d. western section of the circle

3. What color is it suggested that your altar cloth be?
   a. black
   b. white
   c. whatever color is appropriate for the season
   d. what altar cloth?—Witches don't bother with them

4. This black-handled knife may be sharp, but it is not used to cut:
   a. athame
   b. bolline
   c. besom
   d. scimitar

5. This white-handled knife gets to do all the work, from cutting to inscribing:
   a. bodkin
   b. sickle
   c. athame
   d. bolline

6. A Witch's circle cannot be cast without which of the following tools?
   a. athame
   b. besom
   c. wand
   d. Witch

7. In England, the name of this tool is also slang for "female genitalia." It's made up of two separate pieces that, when put together, can be used to cleanse the space:
   a. bolline
   b. besom
   c. scimitar
   d. stang

8. This tool, usually made of natural materials, is used to direct energy. Hermes owned one that was entwined with snakes:
   a. wand
   b. caduceus
   c. stave
   d. staff

9. Traditionally, how long should your wand be cut?
   a. the measure from your mouth to the center of your chest—about ten inches
   b. from your hara (solar plexus) to your root chakra (genitals), about thirteen inches
   c. from your middle finger to your elbow, about eighteen inches
   d. thirteen inches, one for each member of the coven

10. A blasting rod is
    a. a rod used for conducting electricity
    b. something used by a demolition company
    c. a wand used for cursing
    d. a staff or rod for divining, directing energy, or protection

11. This container, used to burn incense, looks like a small cauldron with legs and can sit on the altar:
    a. votive
    b. thurible
    c. censer
    d. crucible

12. In the magic circle, incense is used to
    a. cleanse and charge the space
    b. make the space smell pretty for the worshipers
    c. confuse the evil sprits
    d. give form to the magical barrier

13. Placed toward the back of the altar as a focal point and to remind the worshipers of their connection with the universal powers:
    a. plate of food, usually bread

b. the coven's Book of Shadows

c. parchment paper listing the names of the coveners

d. statues or other representations of the God and Goddess

14. This is traditionally sounded with each invocation in a Wiccan circle as a means of calling the attention of the Gods:
    a. bell
    b. gong
    c. bull's horn
    d. conch shell

15. Symbolizing the presence of the Horned God, a stang is used in Robert Cochrane's form of Witchcraft. It is
    a. a forked wooden staff
    b. a sword
    c. a staff with antlers
    d. a statue of the Horned God

16. A bodkin is a
    a. bowl for incense
    b. bloodletting tool
    c. cloak clasp
    d. special pen for writing in your Book of Shadows

17. Another name for the cord is a
    a. cingulum
    b. rope
    c. twine
    d. noose

18. Which one of these tools is *not* used for assistance in entering an altered state?
    a. drum
    b. cords
    c. stang
    d. scourge

19. Considered by some to be an emblem of a High Priestess, it grows heavier with each Priestess hived:
    a. necklace

b. garter
c. Book of Shadows
d. conscience

20. A five-sided figure drawn while invoking the spirits:
    a. pentagon
    b. pentagram
    c. pentacle
    d. Pentateuch

21. What does a reversed pentacle represent?
    a. energy dissolving into matter
    b. the Horned God
    c. the rank of Second Degree
    d. all of the above

22. Traditionally, what are the five points of the pentacle associated with?
    a. God, king, country, man, woman
    b. earth, air, fire, water, spirit
    c. hops, water, malt, barley, yeast
    d. apple, oak, maple, hawthorn, hazel

23. What is the most powerful representation of fire you can put on your altar?
    a. dragon
    b. wand
    c. lit candle
    d. athame

24. What is the Bell, Book, and Candle ritual?
    a. a calling of the spirits for celebration
    b. a ritual of excommunication
    c. a magical working to create balance with the Witch and the Gods
    d. a self-initiatory ritual

25. What personal item represents the microcosm of the self within the macrocosm of the circle?
    a. armband

b. cingulum

c. bodkin

d. unbroken necklace

26. Why do many Witches like to wear necklaces made from a combination of amber and jet?
    a. they carry an electrical charge
    b. the polarity inherent in their color
    c. they were both formerly living substances
    d. all of the above

27. What is regarded by many as the Witch's most important tool?
    a. athame
    b. wand
    c. matches
    d. sword

28. In some traditions, the acting Priestess may wear a crown with a crescent moon on the front. What can the Priests wear?
    a. crown with a crescent moon
    b. horned crown
    c. crown with a sun
    d. nothing; there is no crown for Priests

29. This is also called "the Witches' Alphabet." It is a form of writing used for inscribing magical objects:
    a. Pictish Script
    b. Minoan sigils
    c. Malachim
    d. Theban Script

30. This runic system of writing was described by Robert Graves in his book *The White Goddess:*
    a. the Tree Alphabet
    b. Pictish Script
    c. Malachim
    d. the Celtic Runes

31. A Book of Shadows is
    a. an ancient book that has been passed down from Witch to Witch since the Middle Ages
    b. a personal diary
    c. a tradition-specific ritual book shared with its initiates
    d. a book on making shadow puppets

32. Sensitive to psychic energy, these pets seem to enjoy working magic with their owners. In contemporary Wicca, they are called
    a. pets
    b. familiars
    c. imps
    d. demons

33. Which of these should not be on the altar?
    a. the cat
    b. candles
    c. the Priestess
    d. chalice

SECTION 2

Within and Without—The Circle

34. Why is the ritual space created in the form of a circle?
    a. because no one likes to have to stand in the corner
    b. because a circle is a reflection of the cosmos and the cycles of rebirth
    c. because it is more difficult to cast a magic square
    d. because Starhawk says we are supposed to

35. The circle is usually cast moving deosil, or in a _____ direction.
    a. from above to below
    b. right to left
    c. counterclockwise
    d. clockwise

36. This term comes from the Anglo-Saxon *with sith,* meaning "to walk against":
    a. counterclockwise
    b. widdershins
    c. clockwise
    d. witherway

37. Why is a circle cast deosil?
    a. it is an ancient tradition, passed down from the Egyptians
    b. it's going with the flow
    c. most people are right-handed, so it's easier to remember to turn right when casting—thus keeping continuity
    d. it's what most people do; why change?

38. For what reason would a circle be cast counterclockwise?
    a. circles are never conjured in a counterclockwise direction
    b. when doing past-life regressions
    c. when working baneful magic, binding and banishing spells
    d. for initiations and elevations

39. The circumference of a Witch's circle is traditionally
    a. six feet
    b. nine feet
    c. twenty-eight feet
    d. twelve feet or as big as is necessary to hold all the participants

40. Once a circle has been cast, how may it be left or entered?
    a. cutting a door
    b. only cats may leave a cast circle without disruption
    c. once a circle is conjured, no one may enter or leave until the rite is ended
    d. osmosis

41. What is the difference between a Witch's circle and a Ceremonial Magician's circle?
    a. the words used to create it
    b. a Witch creates a magical circle to make a connection

with the Gods; a magician's circle is to keep the spirits at bay

c. magicians visualize a purple light; Witches see it as green

d. there are no differences between the two

42. A prescribed order of ceremony to achieve a transformation of consciousness is a
    a. circle
    b. spell
    c. ritual
    d. pathworking

43. What does it mean to be properly prepared?
    a. to be ritually and emotionally ready for ritual
    b. to have received the sacred password
    c. to have gathered and laid out all the necessary tools for the rite
    d. the circle has been cast, the elements invoked, and the participants are emotionally, physically, and psychically ready to work magic

44. Why do initiates choose a magical name?
    a. to confuse the mundanes
    b. because it sounds interesting and unusual
    c. to give the illusion that it is an old and venerable tradition
    d. to help put the practitioner into a magical frame of mind

45. Within a three-degree system, she is usually a Second Degree Witch who assists the High Priestess:
    a. Mother
    b. Maiden
    c. Princess
    d. Lady

46. Another name for the summoner, the person in charge of scheduling and notifying the coven members of meetings, is
    a. fetch
    b. caller

    c. herald

    d. secretary

47. How many people are traditionally in a coven?
    a. three
    b. five
    c. thirteen
    d. the number that can fit in the living room of the coven-stead

48. When you are summoning the presence of a spiritual deity, you are
    a. blessing
    b. conjuring
    c. evoking
    d. invoking

49. To bless something and make it sacred is to
    a. consecrate
    b. saturate
    c. consummate
    d. contaminate

50. The circle is _____ with salt and water; the circle is _____ with fire and air.
    a. made wet; made sweet
    b. charged; cleansed
    c. cleansed; charged
    d. cleansed; cleansed

51. These are symbolic structures that are envisioned standing at the compass points:
    a. fairy mounds
    b. pentagrams
    c. the Watchtowers
    d. bridges

52. How many elements of life are traditionally invoked into the Witch's circle?
    a. four

      b. five

      c. two

      d. none

53. Match up each element with its traditional compass point:

      a. earth   _____   1. east

      b. air   _____   2. west

      c. fire   _____   3. south

      d. water   _____   4. north

54. What element does the center hold?

      a. none—it is the Void

      b. Akasha

      c. crystal

      d. love

55. Elementals are spirits that personify the four elements. Which of the follows is the elemental for earth?

      a. gnomes

      b. trolls

      c. tree spirits

      d. golems

56. Which of the following is the elemental for air?

      a. fairies

      b. birds

      c. sylphs

      d. sprites

57. Which of the following is the elemental for fire?

      a. phoenix

      b. dragon

      c. salamander

      d. naga

58. Which of the following is the elemental for water?

      a. undines

      b. mermaids

      c. dolphins

      d. sea serpents

59. Which of the following pentacles is an earth-invoking pentagram?

a.

b.

c.

d.

60. Which of the following pentacles is a water-banishing pentagram?

a.

b.

c.

d.

61. Which of the following pentacles is an air-invoking pentagram?

a.

b.

c.

d.

62. Which of the following pentacles is a fire-invoking pentagram?

a.

b.

c.

d.

63. Which of the following pentacles is an earth-banishing pentagram?

a.

b.

c.

d.

64. When selecting deities to invoke into your circle, it is important to
    a. select only deities who reflect your own genetic heritage
    b. select deities who don't get along with each other so they have an opportunity to work out their issues and make up
    c. select deities you are knowledgeable about and have a relationship with
    d. select deities you don't know much about so you have a chance to meet them

65. Altered states of consciousness can be obtained through
    a. fasting
    b. physical exertion
    c. chemicals
    d. all of the above

66. If you are using repeated vocal tones to raise energy, you are most likely
    a. yodeling
    b. chanting
    c. annoying your neighbors
    d. suffering from Tourette's syndrome

67. The Great Rite is
    a. a symbolic joining of the male and female principles
    b. a ritual that everyone agrees went extremely well
    c. a turn of 180 degrees
    d. Halloween, the most important seasonal holiday of the Witches

68. This technique can be used by a group to aid in focusing and raising energy through the power of imagination:
    a. meditation
    b. dancing
    c. pathworking
    d. vision quest

69. A grounding is
    a. a spellworking
    b. a ritual for the Earth
    c. working with Earth energy
    d. tapping into the energies of the Earth to become psychically balanced

70. The subtle nonlocalized extension of the physical body is called
    a. an avatar
    b. astral projection
    c. a doppelgänger
    d. an incubus

71. The offering of a gift, especially to a deity, in exchange for a blessing or for giving of thanks is called
    a. sacrifice
    b. libation
    c. tip
    d. advice

72. Some Witches, Pagans, and New Agers develop a relationship with a spirit guide. Just as the name suggests, these spirits help guide the individual toward a heightened level of

spiritual development. Which of these would you most likely want as your spirit guide?
a. your great-grandmother
b. Hunk Ra
c. Sid Vicious
d. an ascended master

73. When the rite has ended, the spirits are thanked and asked to "stay if you will, go if you must . . ." This act is called
a. dismissing
b. banishing
c. excusing
d. placating

SECTION 3

Wiccan and Pagan Seasonal Celebrations and Get-Togethers

74. In modern Paganism, the seasonal celebrations are reflections of the cycles of life, death, and rebirth. These festivals are said to be
a. the buttons on the joystick
b. the stew in the cauldron
c. the circle of life
d. the Wheel of the Year

75. A seasonal Wiccan festival is called
a. a Sabbat
b. an esbat
c. a Shabbat
d. a sexual romp

76. In an average year, there are how many Wiccan seasonal celebrations?
a. four
b. 356
c. eight
d. twelve

77. In an average year, there are how many Full-Moon celebrations?
    a. four
    b. thirteen
    c. eight
    d. twelve

78. What is a blue moon?
    a. the winter full moon
    b. the third full moon in a season when four full moons occur
    c. two full moons occurring within the same month
    d. a bar in Manhattan that serves great margaritas

79. Of the Wiccan Sabbats, how many of them are solar celebrations?
    a. four
    b. two
    c. eight
    d. none; Wiccans follow a lunar calendar

80. What calendar do Wiccans use?
    a. Celtic
    b. Julian
    c. Gregorian
    d. Wiccan

81. Wiccan holidays are traditionally celebrated
    a. from evening through to the following evening
    b. from dawn until dawn the next day
    c. from midnight through the following midnight
    d. from noon until noon the following day

82. At this holiday, we celebrate the return of Kore, the Maiden of Spring:
    a. Ostara
    b. Yule
    c. Mabon
    d. Midsummer

83. This is a Celtic harvest celebration honoring the "first fruits" of the year. At this time, the corn is harvested and thanks are given to the Goddess of the Land for granting the abundance to Her people:
   a. Litha
   b. Fall Equinox
   c. Lammas
   d. Imbolc

84. Another name for midsummer is
   a. Mabon
   b. Litha
   c. Ostara
   d. Samhain

85. The fall equinox is also referred to as
   a. Mabon
   b. Samhain
   c. Yule
   d. Lughnasadh

86. At what point in the seasonal calendar is the sacrifice of John Barleycorn?
   a. Fall Equinox
   b. Beltane
   c. Lammas
   d. Imbolc

87. This is the most significant of the eight Sabbats, because it marks the beginning of the new year for Wiccans and most Pagans:
   a. Yule
   b. Beltane
   c. Samhain
   d. Litha

88. Imbolc, Samhain, Beltane, and Lammas are all derived from
   a. ancient fire festivals
   b. ancient solar festivals

c. modern folk traditions

d. ancient festivals celebrated at Stonehenge

89. In the Celtic world, this Sabbat was also the time when the courts were convened, contracts were signed, and the rents were due to the landlords:
a. Lammas
b. Samhain
c. Litha
d. Yule

90. Which Sabbat takes its name from either the Norse word *hjol*, or the Anglo-Saxon word *hwéol*, both of which mean "wheel"?
a. Lammas
b. Yule
c. Imbolc
d. Beltane

91. This Celtic fertility Goddess has given Her name to both a Pagan seasonal festival and a Christian holiday:
a. Ostara
b. Litha
c. Mabon
d. Epona

92. Which Sabbat's name translates as "in the belly"?
a. Mabon
b. Beltane
c. Imbolc
d. Ostara

93. When the corn is harvested, the last portion of the crop is left standing, because it is said that the spirit of the corn remains in the last sheaf. Once the harvest is in, this last stalk is then
a. ritually cut down with a golden blade and placed on a white sheet to be kept for the next planting
b. ritually cut down and fashioned into a doll

    c. left standing to be sown into the ground the following year

    d. ritually cut down, tied into bundles of three, and hung by the kitchen door for good luck

94. What does the word *Samhain* mean?
    a. slaughter
    b. summer's end
    c. winter's end
    d. rebirth

95. We can still see the remnants of this Roman holiday reflected in our modern celebration of New Year's. The Romans celebrated the death of the old order and the descent into anarchy before the reestablishing of the new:
    a. Lupercalia
    b. Lectisternium
    c. Saturnalia
    d. Cinco de Mayo

96. On the Celtic calendar, this celebration marks the end of winter and the beginning of summer:
    a. Litha
    b. Ostara
    c. Imbolc
    d. Beltane

97. At what point in the seasonal wheel did the Druids harvest the sacred mistletoe that hung upon the oak trees?
    a. midsummer
    b. midwinter
    c. spring equinox
    d. fall equinox

98. Which Sabbat sees the crowning of the May Queen and King, symbols of the divine couple whose sacred union ensures growth and fertility?
    a. Ostara
    b. midsummer

    c. Imbolc

    d. Beltane

99. Which Celtic Goddess is honored by both Pagans and Christians?

    a. Epona

    b. Ceridwen

    c. Bridget

    d. Modron

100. At what time in the year does the Oak King traditionally challenge, fight, and kill the Holly King?

    a. winter solstice

    b. midsummer

    c. fall equinox

    d. spring equinox

The Sabbats

101. Match each Sabbat with its corresponding dates (1 point per correct answer):

A. Ostara _____	1. August 1
B. Mabon _____	2. December 21 or 22
C. Imbolc _____	3. November 1
D. Litha _____	4. September 22 or 23
E. Beltane _____	5. February 2
F. Samhain _____	6. March 21
G. Yule _____	7. May 1
H. Lammas _____	8. June 21 or 22

Answers to Chapter 2

Unless otherwise stated, give yourself *2 points for each correct answer.* Total your points at the end of each section. These totals will be added together at the end of the chapter, giving you a final score for the chapter. This final score will be carried forward to the end of the book for your final count and I.Q. evaluation!

SECTION 1

Tools and Toys

1. C. An altar can be anything—a table, a rock, the top of a dresser. It can be temporary, used only for the duration of your ritual, or permanent, a place for daily focus and personal communion with the spirits and the Gods.

2. B or C. This is tradition-specific or a matter of personal preference. Some prefer the northern realm, because this direction is associated with the element earth, home to the seeds of growth, manifestation, and the mysteries that must be revealed. Others place their altar in the east to face the direction from which the sun and the moon rise.

3. C. This is also a matter of personal preference. Usually people choose colors that reflect the nature of the magical working or the seasonal celebration. Some crafty folks create unique altar cloths of exceptional beauty through the embroidering of magical symbols or the quilting of multicolored fabric. Others don't bother with a cloth at all.

4. A. An athame is a double-edged knife made of iron or steel that is used to cast the circle and direct energy. In order to form a bond with their tool, some Traditions use the athame

as an actual knife, both inside and outside the circle. But most traditions do not use an athame for mundane purposes, believing that it will detract from the magical intention. A few Traditions will destroy the athame if it ever accidentally draws blood—it's believed that this will contaminate the energy.

5. D. The bolline, otherwise known as the white-handled knife, is the working tool of the Witch. It can be used in the circle to inscribe amulets, cut herbs, carve candles, slice the ritual cheese, and so on.

6. D. You can't cast a Witch's circle without a Witch.

7. B. *Besom* is another name for "broom." The materials that make up the broom are often Tradition-specific. Some believe it should be an ash haft with a birch twig spray. Others say any old stick bound with grain that can sweep will do. It represents male and female joined. It is said that the Witches would "ride" the broom, jumping up and down, to show the crops how high to grow. In Wiccan circles, it is used to sweep and cleanse the space.

8. A. A wand is used to direct energy. The wood that the wand is made out of is often Tradition-specific. *The Key of Solomon* suggests that it be of hazel or nut that was harvested at dawn on a Wednesday, the day ruled by Mercury. While some use hazel, wands of ash and willow are also favored by Witches. Just as with the besom, Witches will make theirs out of whatever suits them. I've seen some very expensive wands crafted from metal and encrusted with crystals and gems. Hermes's wand was called a caduceus. Entwined with snakes and with wings on the top, it is still the symbol of healing for the medical profession.

9. C. The measure from your middle finger to elbow, which is about eighteen inches, depending on your size. Again, the wood used is Tradition-specific. It is said that to harvest the

wood properly, it should be cut when the moon is waxing or full and that a proper offering should be left. There are some who offer a drop of their blood, in exchange for the blood that the tree shed.

10. D. According to *Witches: An Encyclopedia of Paganism and Magic* by Michael Jordan, the magical powers of a staff date back to Moses, when he struck his rod upon a rock and a fresh spring erupted (Book of Exodus). Today *blasting rod* refers to a stave or staff that is carried by a Witch. It is used for divining, directing energy, or, if need be, protection.

11. B. A censer has the benefit of a chain so that it can be walked around the circle without burning your fingers on the hot metal. A thurible remains on the altar. The "legs" are to help protect your table and altar cloth.

12. A. Incense is used to charge and cleanse the circle and to send prayers up to the Gods.

13. D. A statue or other representation of the God and Goddess. It is usually an image of the deities who will be invoked into the circle. The coven may, or may not, work with the same pair each esbat or seasonal celebration. Some Traditions have only a figure of a Goddess on their altar.

14. A. The bell is used for this purpose, although some Traditions may use one of the other items listed for special or specific occasions.

15. A. A stang is a forked wooden staff, usually of ash wood. It stands at the northernmost point of the circle, symbolizing the Horned God. It is often decorated to reflect the seasonal celebration.

16. B. Not all Traditions use this tool, but a few do. It is used to produce a very small drop of blood offered as a symbolic sacrifice. For example, when a cutting for a wand has been taken, a drop of blood may be offered to the tree in exchange for its sacrifice.

17. A. A cord is sometimes referred to as a cingulum.

18. C. A stang is Robert Cochrane's forked staff. As with any type of focal point, if you stare at it long enough it could act as tool to alter consciousness, but this isn't its primary use. All the others are tools listed are usually used in some way to alter states of consciousness.

19. B. The green garter is considered an emblem of rank. The High Priestess adds a silver buckle to the garter for each coven that has hived off her own. Not all Priestesses practice this tradition—some would have so many buckles attached that, due to the weight, she would have difficulty keeping it from sliding down her leg.

20. C. A lot of people get this one wrong. A pentagon is a five-sided object. The Pentateuch is the books of Moses. A pentagram is a geometric device that is written or drawn, such as when invoking the spirits. It is a five-pointed star made up of five straight lines. A pentacle is a pentagram, a five-pointed star, but it is inscribed onto a disk made of wood, metal, clay, wax, or earthenware and has a circle around it. If you are wearing a necklace with a five-pointed star, you are wearing a pentacle. It represents Earth on the altar. Confused? You're not the only one. Over time, *pentacle* and *pentagram* have come to be used interchangeably.

21. D. In Wicca, the reversed pentacle is the symbol of the Horned God of the Wild Hunt and Nature. In some Traditions, it is the symbol of the Second Degree initiation. The top point of a pentacle represents spirit. When the point is positioned downward, toward the Earth, it can symbolize the transformation of energy to the physical plane.

22. B. Earth, air, fire, water, and spirit are the most common associations with the points of the pentacle. As in the Faerie Tradition, however, many energies—from the cycles of life to the powers of the Witch—can also be correlated with the points of this magical symbol.

23. C. The most powerful representation of something is the item itself. Therefore, although all the items listed can be used as symbols of fire, the candle flame is the correct answer. Candles are also as a visual representation of spirits invoked into the circle.

24. B. This is a phrase from the Roman Catholic ritual for excommunication from the church. Very ironic when you realize that the church was in effect doing the exact same thing of which they were accusing others—casting a curse!

25. D. A continuous necklace is an unbroken circle. It symbolizes the circle and cycles of life. Necklaces are also popular items to empower with magical intent.

26. D. Both amber and jet are parts of trees that were transformed into stone. Amber is fossilized resin, while jet is bituminous wood that is a highly compressed form of carbon. Rub them together and they will generate static electricity! The light amber and the black of the jet, alternated, represent polarity and the cycles of birth and death. Within the Gardnerian or Gardnerian-derived Traditions, a necklace of amber and jet is worn only by those who have attained the rank of Third Degree.

27. A. The athame is regarded by many as the Witch's most important tool. It is placed upon the altar at the gathering of the coven. The sword can act as an athame, but it is harder to use for most ritual activities.

28. B or C. Yes, this is another one of those Tradition-specific things. Most common is a horned crown or helmet, especially during those times when he is representing the Horned God. The sun crown, balancing the moon energy of the Priestess, is an alternative used by some traditions.

29. D. There is some question about when it was created. Some claim that is was during the Middle Ages; others say the script is more modern. Either way, it has become a popular tool for inscribing an object with intent.

30. A. Allegedly of Celtic origins, the Tree Alphabet is described by Robert Graves in his book *The White Goddess*. Each tree was given a mystical association and used as the basis of a runic alphabet. He also called it Beth-Luis-Nion (BLN).

31. C. A Book of Shadows (often referred to as the B.O.S.) is a book filled with rituals, herbal lore, incantations, chants, spells, divination methods, and other miscellaneous writings. There is no one definitive Book of Shadows. Often a Tradition will share a common book, which is then added to or adapted by each individual coven. In addition, each Witch may have a personal and private book.

32. B. Familiars were once considered low-ranking demons who had been sent by the devil to serve the Witch. In contemporary Wicca, it is usually a pet that has chosen to add its energies to those of the owner to work magic. Animals, and young children, have a natural ability to walk into and out of a circle without breaking the energy.

33. A. With candles, cup, burning incense, athame, and other tools that could pose problems for twitching tails, altars don't make good spots for the cat. In some Traditions, the Priestess actually does take a seat upon the altar as a symbol of the Goddess incarnate.

 TOTAL YOUR POINTS
Chapter 2, Section 1: Tools and Toys

_____ Total number of questions 1–33 answered correctly

Multiply your total number of questions 1–33 answered correctly by 2. This will give you your total number of points for chapter 2, section 1:

_____ X 2 = _____

Total number of questions,   Total   score,   chapter   2,
1–33 answered correctly   section 1

(For example: 10 correct. 10 x 2 = a total of 20 points for chapter 2, section 1.)

Total possible points for chapter 2, section 1 = 66

SECTION 2

Within and Without—The Circle

34. B. A circle is a reflection of the cycles of the seasons of life. It is the sun, the moon, the Earth, and the universe. By casting a circle, a Witch is creating a microcosm reflecting the macrocosm of the universe.

35. D. Clockwise or sunwise direction.

36. B. *Widdershins* comes from the term *with sith,* meaning "to walk against." We use the term to indicate counterclockwise or against the natural flow.

37. B. This is the direction that the sun, the Earth, and the moon move. It is the movement of the Earth around the sun, of the passage of light across the planet. A circle is cast with the natural flow of the energy, moving in the same direction as the sun.

38. C. Widdershins can be used in casting a circle for the purpose of working baneful magic, binding and banishing spells. These types of magical workings are counter to the natural flow, therefore a widdershins (counterclockwise) cast is appropriate. Most Wiccan Traditions do not condone any type of baneful magic, so a widdershin circle is not often used.

39. C. The circumference is approximately twenty-eight feet—

the diameter is nine feet! And here is that special number three again. In this case, three times three equals nine.

40. A. Casting a circle creates an energy barrier around the magical space for the purpose of containing and amplifying the energies within. You can't just walk into and out of it; doing so would cause a disruption in the flow and, on a purely emotional level, break the ritual mind-set for the participants. A doorway must be cut in a widdershins motion with an athame or sword to temporarily redirect the flow so that a person can step into or out of the circle. Think of it as sticking your hand into a running brook and gently guiding the water around and away from a rock as compared to putting up a dam.

41. B. A Witch's circle forms a protective space that is said to be between the worlds of the spirits and the worlds of form. The spirits and Gods are then invited inside the circle to work or communicate with the Witch. A Magician's circle acts as a protective space from the powers that are conjured outside of the circle. A Magician stays within his or her circle, which is traditionally inscribed with magical symbols and words of protection, and the spirits are invoked outside it. The circle keeps the spirits at bay so that the Magician, safe within the protected space, can control them.

42. C. Ritual is the form or structure of ceremony, created in a way such that you know on both a conscious and an unconscious level that something special is happening, or will happen. A ritual is used to bring about desired things or changes in consciousness, from summoning the spirits or the deities to working magic and honoring seasonal changes. Wiccan ritual form is a matter of taste, Tradition, and training—and, not surprisingly, a point of argument.

43. D. What it means to be properly prepared will be different for each Tradition. It may include taking a ritual bath, spending some time alone in contemplation, cleaning the ritual space and setting up the altar, receiving words or

phrases necessary for the rite, or connecting with coveners through conversation or loving silence. But the bottom line is that the participants are physically (do not need to use the bathroom, are feeling well, are in appropriate ritual clothing), emotionally (have put aside the fight they had with their lover as well as the stress from their jobs or lives), and psychically (have quieted their minds and are open to the energies around them) ready to welcome the Gods and work magic.

44. D. The idea of a magical name is not new. There are stories and myths about the power in secret names. It is said that, if they fall into the wrong hands, these secret words and names can be used to control the individual for either ill or good. Some folks take a name at initiation to mark their new birth. These names are usually a reflection of their personality or interests, or are intended to draw a particular form of energy to them. In some circles, Craft names are taken to keep confidentiality. The story goes that the reason for a Craft name was so if a Witch was caught by the Inquisition, he or she would not be able to give up the names of those in the coven. Today, a Craft name can be used to help put a person into a magical frame of mind. It is a key word that indicates to your subconscious that you are participating in something special, not ordinary.

Unfortunately, there are those within the community who feel they must change their name as frequently as their socks. I knew one gentleman who changed his name a total of five times in one weekend! I go by the rule of three—you have three chances to change your name. Change it a fourth time and it reverts permanently back to either your original, mundane name or one of my choosing, which I can assure you that you won't like.

45. B. In those Traditions that work with this structure, Maiden is a woman, usually Second Degree Witch, who is the assistant to the High Priestess. Despite the title, she can be of any age. The Maiden substitutes for the High Priestess in

certain tasks, and she also handles various administrative duties such as keeping the training materials in order, keeping track of addresses and phone numbers, and the like. She is also likely to help in the training of initiates.

46. A. *Fetch* is another name for the summoner. He or she is in charge of scheduling meetings and notifying the members of dates, times, locations, and if anything special needs to be brought to the rite. This is another of those titles that is Tradition-specific.

47. C. The idea that a coven was made up of thirteen people most likely came from the minds of the Inquisitors. They believed that Witches worshiped the devil with rites that were an obscene parody of the church. Therefore, a coven must be made up of thirteen people—twelve plus a leader or the devil. This is a corruption of Jesus and his twelve apostles. While traditionally the number thirteen is still considered ideal—and ironically, it is the number that can fit comfortably in a nine-foot circle—modern covens range from three to twenty people, because more or less than this seems to have negative effects upon the group's energy and dynamics. Too many, and getting ready for circle is like herding cats; scheduling a time for esbats becomes a nightmare.

48. D. To *invoke,* according to *Webster's Dictionary,* is "to call for with earnest desire; to call on a deity." We call to the spirits and to the Gods and ask them to come and join us in our circle, to help us in our workings, and to celebrate with us in our joy. An invoking pentagram is drawn as the element is summoned, bringing in positive energy.

49. A. To consecrate is to bless and declare something sacred.

50. C. The circle is cleansed with salt and water; the circle is charged with fire and air. Salt water is the representation of the womb of life, the ocean from which all life emerged. Salt is said to have purifying properties in that it draws out nega-

tive energies, just as salt water can draw out an infection from a wound. Water is refreshing and cleansing. Salt is a symbol of Earth, and water is a symbol of water. Both are considered feminine and receptive principles. Fire is the symbol of fire, and incense represents air. These two elements are considered to be male and hold active principles. This the reason that fire and air (in the form of burning incense) charges, rather than purifies, the circle.

51. C. The Watchtowers are not physical towers. They reflect the four aspects of consciousness and the four cardinal directions.

52. A. This is another one of those Tradition-specific answers. In general, there are four elements invoked into the circle. These four elements make up the building blocks of Nature and are the foundation of natural magic. They are the elements of life; it is believed that they bind us all together with the greater web of humanity, Nature, and the Gods.

53. A—4; B—1; C—3; D—2. All four must be matched to get the points!

54. B. *Akasha* makes up the fifth point on the pentacle, the spirit or center from which all the elements are joined. Borrowed from Hindu, it refers to a dimension of space related by vibration or sound.

55. A. Elementals are the spirits, or Nature spirits, that personify the four elements. They may be summoned to ask for assistance in magic. Gnomes traditionally look like little old men. They live underground and are associated with earth.

56. C. Sylphs are slender and graceful beings who live in the air. They are associated with the element air.

57. C. According to the stories, salamanders live in the flames. Of course, we know they would much prefer to live under a nice, moist tree stump. They are associated with fire because they look like little dragons.

58. A. Undines are water spirits. They appear as beautiful young maidens and are associated with the element water.

59. C.

60. B.

61. B.

62. A.

63. D.

64. C. You would usually try to find something out about strangers before inviting them into your home. The same goes with your circle. Some deities must be approached in very specific ways and can get insulted if you do not provide them with what they are accustomed to. This is similar to asking folks over for dinner and serving them meat when they are vegetarians. You also wouldn't invite a couple over knowing they just completed a very messy and bitter divorce. They won't get along just because you ask them to! Some individuals and traditions prefer to work with only those deities of one specific pantheon, but many mix and match depending upon the seasonal festival or magic needed. For example, you wouldn't ask Mars to help with love magic. Nor would you summon Kore, the Maiden of Spring, at Yule. She'd be cold and grumpy. Remember, the library is your friend. Books on mythology are readily available. Do some research before opening the door to trouble.

65. D. There are many, many ways to enter into a trance or altered state of consciousness—drumming, dancing, meditation, breathwork, chanting, and restriction of motion, to name just a few. Cultures throughout the world and time have used the trance as a means of gaining insight and for communicating with the Gods who exist on those alternate planes. Some can enter into a light hypnotic state very easily, while others need a bit of help from substances such as peyote or alcohol.

66. B. *Chanting* refers to rhythmic and repeated vocal tones. It can be nonsense words or just tones, or an actual song can be repeated over and over. It's a wonderful way to raise energy, especially with a group, because it also acts as a means of synchronizing the coven's breathing, a benefit when working magic.

67. A. The Great Rite is the symbolic joining of the God and Goddess, the divine male and female principles. The chalice and the athame or wand are combined, signifying the sacred joining.

68. C. A pathworking, also called guided meditation, is a technique of using active visualization to bring together the collective minds and energies of the coven. It is facilitated through the narration of an inner journey, into which the participants project themselves.

69. D. The purpose of a grounding is to align your energies with those of the Earth, drawing upon the energy of the Earth and releasing and negative energy back to Her. It is reestablishing the natural flow of energy.

70. B. Astral projection is when you take a trip but leave your body behind. The root of *astral* is the Latin *astum,* meaning "the stars" or "heavenly body." When you astral project, you are flying among the stars. Some people think of the astral plane as being the land of dreams. It is not an easy skill to develop; it takes a lot of time and determination to master.

71. A. Wiccans do not sacrifice humans or animals, but we do make sacrifices. The most common of these are offerings of food, drink, the first fruits of the harvest, and the like. A sacrifice can be a petition—"I'll give you this, if you do that for me." It may be an offering as an appeasement—"I screwed up, I'm sorry." Or it may be in the form of giving thanks— "Thank you, Mom! You're the greatest!"

72. D. A spirit guide is a spirit, sometimes referred to as an as-

cended master, who is there to help you learn your spiritual lessons and guide you on your spiritual path. An ascended master is a spirit who has chosen not to evolve but remains on the astral plane to help other souls who are still in physical form. Not everyone chooses to work with spirit guides. Some prefer those in the flesh. But for those who do, it would be best to work with a spirit who will be able to help teach you. Your great-grandmother may have been a wonderful woman, but how spiritually advanced was she? She might be able to instruct you on making a wonderful peach pie, but will that lead to enlightenment?

73. B. Traditionally, it is called banishing. This word bothers a lot of people, because it implies that you are kicking the elements and deities out of the circle. The same applies to the word *dismissing,* which reminds many of what you would do with a servant. Many Witches now prefer and use the word *devoking* (the opposite of *invoking*).

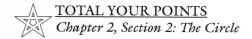

TOTAL YOUR POINTS
Chapter 2, Section 2: The Circle

_____ Total number of questions 34–73 answered correctly

Multiply your total number of questions answered correctly by 2. This will give you your total number of points for chapter 2, section 2:

_____ X 2 = _____

Total number of questions   Total score for chapter 2,
34–73 answered correctly   section 2

Total possible points for chapter 2, section 2 = 80

SECTION 3

Wiccan and Pagan Seasonal Celebrations and Get-Togethers

74. D. The image of a wheel is a very popular way of viewing the cycles. The wheel is something that is ever turning, just as the seasons are forever moving forward.

75. A. The term *Sabbat* is taken from the vocabulary given to us by the Inquisition in Europe. Some Witches are moving away from this word, prefering instead to use something that does not have as many negative associations.

76. C. While every day is a celebration, there are eight Sabbat seasonal festivals in a year.

77. B. In an average year, there are thirteen full-moon cycles, or about one every twenty-eight days . . . give or take a few hours. *Mensis* is Latin for "month" and *mensura* is "measurement." Put it together and you get the monthly, often lunar-influenced, natural cycles of a woman's body.

78. B. Many people believe that a blue moon is when two full moons occur within the same month. Without pointing fingers, this was a misprint in a magazine a number of years ago that was picked up and quoted by a number of other sources. In actuality, a blue moon is the third full moon in a season when four full moons occur. Between spring equinox and midsummer, then, there are normally three full moons. If four occur, then the third one would be the blue moon.

79. A. Four of the Sabbats recognize the actual cycles of the sun. They are the winter and summer solstices and the fall and spring equinoxes. Some Witches will say eight in that they base their calculations for the other Sabbats on the solstices or equinoxes. Some people will use a combination of moon and sun calendars to set the time to celebrate the cross quarters. But the overwhelming majority of Wiccans

and Pagans use the traditional calendar, and covener avail-
ability, to set their celebrations.

80. C. Pope Gregory XIII replaced the Julian calendar in
1582. His new and improved calendar corrected a small
error in calculation of Julius Caesar's version. This new system was not quickly adopted by the populace. In fact, it was
not until 1917—when Russia finally adopted the system—
that it was recognized worldwide.

81. A. Similar to Jewish tradition, the Sabbats are celebrated
from twilight to twilight. For example, Samhain is actually
November 1 and is celebrated on the evening of October
31.

82. A. Kore/Persephone and Her mother Demeter are at the
heart of the Eleusinian mysteries. Each fall, Persephone
must make Her yearly return to the underworld, where She
rules as queen. Come spring, She returns to the surface as
Kore, the Maiden of Spring. The laughter of children as
they dance on the new, wet grass and the planting of seeds
are all a part of the joy found in Kore's return.

83. C. Lammas is the first harvest festival. The first grains,
berries, and other fruits of the lands are collected and thanks
are given to the lady of the land for granting the harvest.

84. B. There is some debate as to how the name *Litha* became
associated with the equinox. It is possible that it came from
Lithe, out of Tolkien's hobbit festival in *Lord of the Rings*.
Others say that it has old Anglo-Saxon roots and point to
Bebe, a writer of the Old English period who used the word
litha for the June-through-July period. Either way, the
name may be old but the usage is possibly modern.

85. A. This is another name that comes with much debate. The
name *Mabon* does not appear to have been associated with
the equinox until the twentieth century. Mabon may have
been taken from a story in the Mabinogian, a book of Welsh
mythology that dates back to the fourteenth century. He ap-

pears as a youth, son of a Earth-type mother. He may have been associated with hunting and fishing. *The Green Egg*, a Pagan magazine, is the first known publication to use the term *Mabon* (in the mid-1970s) to refer to the equinox. This is another case in which the name might be old, but the usage is completely modern.

86. C. John Barleycorn, along with many of the other sacrificial and reborn Gods, is cut down at his prime in August. Of course, the actual timing for the harvest will depend upon geographic location!

87. C. Samhain is the Wiccan and Pagan new year. The harvest is in, and the culling of the herds for winter has begun. We give thanks for what we have and hope that it will be enough to carry through the winter. At Samhain, the veil that separates the world of the living and the spirits of the dead is said to be very thin. It is a time for remembering and honoring our ancestors, the past generations whose existence gave us life.

88. A. These four are based upon the ancient Celtic fire celebrations. Being fire rites, large bonfires were lit for sympathetic magic—either to call back the sun or to keep the fires burning while we wait for its return. For protection of the herds, cattle were often driven between two bonfires at Beltane and Samhain.

89. A. As the harvest is brought in, it's time to settle debts and give the landowners their due.

90. B. Yule, the winter solstice, represents the wheel of the sun rising, signaling the beginning of the seasonal cycle of waxing light.

91. A. *Easter* is also an adaptation of Her name. Did you ever wonder what rabbits and eggs had to do with Easter, the celebration of the Christian reborn God? Nothing! These are the Goddess Ostara's symbols, and are still remembered at Her time of year.

92. C. *Imbolc* is a Celtic term meaning "lactation." It refers to the beginning of the lactation among the ewes as they prepare for the birth of their young, the first sign of the promise of spring's return.

93. B. The sheaves are fashioned into dolls, also called the Corn Mother, Harvest Mother, Corn Maiden or Kirn-baby (which means "corn" in Gaelic), or, more commonly, corn dolly. This dolly was thought to have magical powers of fertility.

94. B. Summer's end.

95. C. The traditions of gift giving, especially of candles, and celebrational debauchery are still evident in our celebrations of Christmas and New Year's. Saturnalia was a harvest festival dedicated to Saturn that ran from approximately December 17 through December 23. Lupercalia occurred on February 15. It is a celebration of Lupercus, the God of the wolves. For some, Cinco de Mayo may include self-indulgence, but it's on the wrong continent (South America) and month (it's the celebration of the fifth of May).

96. D. Beltane! Ostara is the spring equinox. May 1, Beltane, is the beginning of summer (even if it still feels cold and wet).

97. A. Using a golden sickle, they would catch it in a white cloth, never allowing it to touch the ground—the Earth could take the energy of the mistletoe back into Her, leaving the herb useless for magical workings. Mistletoe found growing on oak trees, a sacred tree, was considered to be the most potent.

98. D. The tradition of crowning a May King and May Queen has been ongoing for many, many years. On my last trip to England, I saw in one small town a huge rock used in their May celebrations. On top there was a stone throne. On the front were carved the names of the May Queens dating back to the 1930s and up to that current year. Of course, the tradition goes back much farther than is listed on the stone!

99. C. February 1 is listed on the Christian calendar as St. Bridget's or Bride's day. She is honored either as a nun who founded a convent in Kildare, Ireland, or as "Christ's Milkmaid." Bridget originally was an important Celtic Goddess of healing/midwifery, smithcraft/firecraft, and poetry/inspiration. She is celebrated at the festival of Imbolc, February 1, which is around the time the ewes begin to lactate—the first sign of spring's return.

100. A. The Holly King represents the waning light, the dark of the winter. He battles his brother the Oak King, who represents the sun renewed, at the winter solstice. The Holly King is beaten, and with the winter defeated, the sun's strength returns, bringing with it the lengthening of the days. But the Holly King will be reborn to challenge and kill the Oak King at midsummer, heralding again the return of winter.

The Sabbats

101. Match each Sabbat with its corresponding date (*1 point* per correct match):

A.	Ostara	6	March 21
B.	Mabon	4	September 22 or 23
C.	Imbolc	5	February 2
D.	Litha	8	June 21 or 22
E.	Beltane	7	May 1
F.	Samhain	3	November 1
G.	Yule	2	December 21 or 22
H.	Lammas	1	August 1

TOTAL YOUR POINTS
Chapter 2, Section 3: The Seasonal Celebrations

_____Total number of 2-point questions, 74–100, answered correctly

Multiply your total number of questions 74–100 answered correctly by 2. This will give you your total number of points for chapter 2, section 3:

_____ X 2 = _____
Total number of 2-point questions   Total number of points
74–100 answered correctly   for questions 74–100

_____ Total number of 1-point matches, question 101

Add together your 2-point question total with your 1-point question total

_____ + _____ = _____
1-point total,   2-point total,   Total score,
question 101   questions 74–100   chapter 2, section 3

Total possible points for chapter 2, section 3 = 62

TOTALING CHAPTER 2

Add together your final scores from each section in Chapter 2:

_____ Chapter 2, section 1—Tools and Toys
+ _____ Chapter 2, section 2—Within and Without—The Circle
+ _____ Chapter 2, section 3—Seasonal Celebrations

= [   ] Grand total for chapter 2

   This is the number you will carry forward to the end of the book!

Total possible points for chapter 2 = 208

Which Witch Is Which?
The History of the Witch

The past, both joyful and painful, must not be forgotten. These prior lives and experiences have brought Witches to where we are today: fighting the labels created over the centuries, embracing a new and wonderful present, and looking toward the future with hope and trepidation. The broom closet that many have hid in for so long is creaking open, and the Witches are returning to the land. For the first time since ancient days, we, the magic workers who worship the Earth and all upon it, are slowly being recognized again, not as some strange creatures who need to be healed but as healers. Yet there is still fear among many Witches and Pagans that ignorance and fundamentalism will again demand to dance with us, and the past will become our present.

Both those who faced the Inquisitions and those who were members of the jury condemning Witches were our ancestors. Without their breath of existence, we would not be here to experience this moment. The majority of those who died with the label of Witch faced their God while speaking Christian prayers. They may not have been magic workers, or they may have known and practiced the healing arts. Either way, they died because they were believed to be Witches, a title that many Wiccans hold proudly. In some cases, such as among those who were executed during the

Salem witch hysteria, they could have saved themselves if they'd confessed to being a Witch. Instead, they faced the gallows rather than admit to a lie and give up their convictions. I would like to believe that if I were faced with the same situation, I would stand as proudly and strongly for my own beliefs. I honor those accused, and remember them. They may not have been Witches in the same sense, but I embrace them as my ancestors.

SECTION 1

Witchcraft in the Ages

1. The earliest form of Witchcraft was most likely
   a. tribal Shamanism
   b. temple Priestesses
   c. divination experts
   d. village wise women

2. For centuries, many came to hear the words of these Priestesses. Armies would not move and important decisions would not be made without first consulting
   a. the Witch
   b. the Vestal Virgins
   c. the Strega
   d. the Oracle of Delphi

3. Written by Apuleius in the second century C.E., this is one of the earliest fictional accounts of witchcraft:
   a. *Pygmalion*
   b. *The Golden Bough*
   c. *The Golden Ass*
   d. *The Odyssey*

4. Based on the original writings of the Hebrew Bible, the followers of the God Yahweh believed that "Thou shalt not suffer_____ to live."
   a. a witch
   b. a medium

    c. an evil spell-caster
    d. a Goddess worshiper

5. With the initial conversion of Europe to Christianity, the number of people accused and killed as witches
    a. increased slightly
    b. increased sharply
    c. remained the same
    d. decreased

6. This ecclesiastical document, recorded in 900 C.E., defined witchcraft as devil worship but also declared it was nothing more than foolish delusion:
    a. the Reformation
    b. the Papal Reform Movement
    c. Nicene Creed
    d. the Canon Episcopi

7. His philosophy about witches laid the foundation for years of persecution at the hands of the Inquisition. His writings influenced the church's view toward sorcery, moving it away from the Canon Episcopi and in the direction of witchcraft being labeled a heresy:
    a. Pope Leo IX
    b. Thomas Aquinas
    c. Tomás de Torquemada
    d. Pope Urban II

8. Reginald Scot (1538–1599) is remembered as the author of *The Discoverie of Witchcraft*, in which he
    a. questioned beliefs about witches and opposed witch hunters
    b. produced a list of methods for uncovering and prosecuting witchcraft
    c. proved that witches are part of a Nature religion that worships a Goddess
    d. described a golden box that holds all the knowledge of the witch, hidden until sanity returns to the land

9. Written by Agrippa during the sixteenth century, this book, a three-volume work titled *On Occult Philosophy*, had an enormous effect on the development of Western occult thought. Which of the following summarizes the philosophies found within the work?
   a. there is no connection between the devil and magic
   b. magic depends on natural psychic gifts
   c. the highest power is found within Nature
   d. all of the above

10. Jules Michelet (1798–1874) was a French historian and author of *La Sorciere*. He was the first European writer to
    a. put forth the modern theory that Witches were the surviving remains of a pre-Christian Nature religion led by Priestesses
    b. combine ceremonial magic with folk traditions
    c. write a nonfiction book that portrayed the witch as a sympathetic and romantic character
    d. put magical theories to test by holding mass "power circles" for change

11. This club was opened by Sir Francis Dashwood in the eighteenth century. Known for its debauchery, it included such distinguished names as Benjamin Franklin on its member list:
    a. the Friarwood Club
    b. the Woodcroft Club
    c. the Hellfire Club
    d. the Real Men Club

12. This medieval term is a common word describing someone who works with folk magic, herbs, and divination, as well as creating counterspells:
    a. cunning person
    b. hedge witch
    c. peller
    d. witch

SECTION 2

You Have the Right to Remain Silent—
Witchcraft and the Law

13. There have been laws passed prohibiting the practice of witchcraft or spellcraft for malignant ends since
    a. Constantine
    b. the Christianization of Europe
    c. ancient Rome
    d. William the Conqueror

14. Who passed the first statute against witchcraft in England, allowing the civil courts to try and punish witches?
    a. James I
    b. Edward IV
    c. Henry VIII
    d. Henry I

15. Which king passed the Witchcraft Act of 1604, and why did he hate witches?
    a. Edward VI; a coven refused to let him join
    b. Richard II; he believed they were spying on him
    c. Henry V; he wanted a horse, they gave him a cow
    d. James I (of England), James VI (of Scotland); he believed a coven was working malicious magic toward him

16. How did the Witchcraft Act of 1604 differ from the earlier witchcraft acts?
    a. the 1604 act distinguished between, and allowed for, the practice of "good" magic
    b. the 1604 act was more lenient than the previous law, allowing for retribution
    c. the 1604 act was considerably stricter in its punishment of witches
    d. there was little difference between the two

17. The 1604 Witchcraft Act in England was repealed in 1736, but a new law was put into its place. This new law

  a. punished those who claimed to possess magical powers
     with prison time of up to one year and public humiliation
  b. repealed the death penalty but replaced it with life in
     prison
  c. required the payment of hefty penalty fees if caught prac-
     ticing magic
  d. eliminated confession through torture

18. Helen Duncan, a known medium, is often cited as being the
    last person charged and imprisoned in England under the
    1735 Witchcraft Act. On what grounds was she charged?
    a. reading Tarot cards
    b. indecency
    c. having violated security laws
    d. malicious magic

19. The 1736 Witchcraft laws were repealed in 1951 and re-
    placed with what is the current law in England. This law is
    called
    a. there was no new law; it was just completely removed
       from the books
    b. the Anti-Witchcraft Act
    c. the Fraudulent Mediums Act
    d. Unlawful-Love Act

20. When were the witchcraft laws removed from the federal
    statute books in the United States?
    a. 1948
    b. 1951
    c. 1980
    d. there was never a federal law against witchcraft

SECTION 3

The Blood of the Ancients—
The Burning Times[1]

21. What time period is traditionally called by Witches "the Burning Times"?
    a. early fourteenth through eighteenth centuries
    b. mid–fourteenth through seventeenth centuries
    c. mid–fifteenth through eighteenth centuries
    d. late sixteenth through nineteenth centuries

22. When was the peak for witch trials?
    a. 1550–1650
    b. 1600–1700
    c. 1450–1600
    d. 1700–1800

23. The vast majority of witches who died were condemned by
    a. the church courts—the Inquisition
    b. the localized secular courts
    c. the national secular government courts—the king's court
    d. none of the above

24. What is the inquisition?
    a. a law of action put forth from the church
    b. a strong arm of the Catholic Church
    c. a type of trial used throughout Europe
    d. a point of secular law

25. The Inquisition was a campaign to eradicate
    a. pagans
    b. witches
    c. heretics
    d. midwives

[1]The majority of information on the Burning Times comes from Gibbons, Jenny. "Recent Developments in the Study of the Great European Witch Hunt." *The Pomegranate, A New Journal of Neopagan Thought* 5 (August 1998), pp. 2–16. She and other scholars focusing on the Witch hunts are changing our perceptions about our history.

26. Heresy is
    a. any deviation from orthodoxy
    b. practice of another religion
    c. bearing false witness
    d. Goddess worship

27. What did Pope Innocent IV do to help open the way for the Burning Times?
    a. allowed for the confiscation of a convicted heretic's possessions
    b. gave permission to torture accused witches
    c. labeled witches as heretics
    d. ordered that all witches must be burned at the stake

28. Pope Innocent VIII's papal bull delivered his deadly edict in 1484. This bull was issued
    a. as a means to eliminate all witches
    b. to quell Protestant opposition and target witches as heretics
    c. to stop midwives and healers from practicing their trades
    d. as an order to priests to report all suspected heretics to the civil authorities

29. What Christian sect made up the papal Inquisition and Inquisitors?
    a. Dominicans
    b. Franciscans
    c. Carmelites
    d. Augustinians

30. The *Malleus Maleficarum* (1486) is also called
    a. the Malicious Magic of Witches
    b. the Witches' Hammer
    c. the bloody book
    d. the devil's book

31. The *Malleus* was reproduced numerous times over the years. How often was it reprinted before being discontinued?
    a. sixteen editions

b. twenty editions
c. thirty editions
d. it is still available

32. Who was/were the author(s) of the *Malleus Maleficarum*?
    a. Heinrich Kramer and Jakob Sprenger
    b. Ozzie and Harriet
    c. Pope Innocent VIII
    d. Aleister Crowley

33. During what historical event did the number of witchcraft trials increase dramatically?
    a. the Christian conversion of Europe, about 500 C.E.
    b. the Black Plague, in 1347–1349 C.E.
    c. the papal bull against witchcraft in 1484 C.E.
    d. the split between the Protestant and Catholic Churches, called the Reformation, of 1550 C.E.

34. Using torture, lies, deceit, and fraud, he was England's most notorious professional Witch hunter:
    a. Cotton Mather
    b. Heinrich Kramer
    c. Jakob Sprenger
    d. Matthew Hopkins

35. Most people accused of witchcraft were
    a. Witches
    b. Christians
    c. midwives
    d. Pagans

36. Those who accused the "white" witch or healer of witch-craft were often[2]
    a. doctors
    b. other healers
    c. the patients
    d. all of the above

[2]This question is based on one from Jenny Gibbons. "Recent Developments in the Study of the Great European Witch Hunt: The Great Burning Times Quiz." *The Pomegranate, A New Journal of Neopagan Thought* 5 (August 1998), p. 3.

37. Recent scholarly work places the number of people executed
     during the Inquisitions to be around
     a. fifty to sixty thousand
     b. 150,000 to 200,000
     c. half a million to one million
     d. nine million

38. Of those accused, _____ percent were women, but in some
     countries up to _____ percent were men.[3]
     a. 50 percent; 60 percent
     b. 80 percent; 90 percent
     c. 100 percent; 10 percent
     d. 75 percent; 40 percent

39. If you were standing before the Spanish Inquisition accused
     of being a _____ , chances are you would be condemned.
     a. Protestant
     b. Witch
     c. Pagan
     d. Jew

40. Which country had the highest rate of witch executions?
     a. Germany
     b. Spain
     c. Ireland
     d. England

41. Which country, of those that held witch trials, had the low-
     est number of executions?
     a. Scotland
     b. Switzerland
     c. Ireland
     d. England

[3]Gibbons, p.13.

SECTION 4

Witchcraft Is a Hanging Offense— The Witch Hysteria in the U.S.

42. What was the actual site where the witchcraft hysteria of 1692 began?
    a. Danvers
    b. Andover
    c. Salem
    d. Winchester

43. What was the name of the Reverend Parris's servant who taught the girls in the neighborhood forms of divination that, perhaps, inadvertently began the witch hysteria?
    a. Tituba
    b. Tabitha
    c. Samantha
    d. Eudora

44. Who were the first accused as witches?
    a. Sarah Wilds and Elizabeth How
    b. Sarah Osborne and Sarah Good
    c. Elizabeth Proctor
    d. Abigail Williams and Ann Putnam

45. The proof of guilt during the Salem trials was almost completely based upon
    a. physical evidence
    b. testimony of neighbors
    c. spectral evidence
    d. spectral and physical evidence

46. Who was the first to die during the Salem witch trials?
    a. Bridget Bishop
    b. Elizabeth Proctor
    c. Rebecca Nurse
    d. George Burroughs

47. Despite his involvement with the Salem witch trials, he was skeptical about spectral evidence and cautioned the judges not to place too much emphasis on it:
    a. Nathaniel Hawthorne
    b. Cotton Mather
    c. Justice Stoughton
    d. the Reverend Noyes

48. Of the following, who was not condemned and hung as a witch?
    a. George Jacobs
    b. Mary Esty
    c. Giles Corey
    d. Sarah Good

49. There were ____ people accused and ____ people executed during the Salem witch trials.
    a. 50; 8
    b. 96; 13
    c. 160; 19
    d. 250; 26

50. What finally put a stop to the Salem trials?
    a. the girls accused the wife of the governor
    b. Ann Putnam Jr. admitted that she had lied
    c. the girls were sued for slander
    d. after the death of the Reverend George Burroughs, the town stopped believing the girls and things just stopped on their own

SECTION 5

Give Me That Old-Time Religion—
The Modern Magical Movement

51. Who published the first book that included wording later incorporated into the Charge of the Goddess?
    a. Charles Leland
    b. Doreen Valiente

    c. Gerald Gardner

    d. Aleister Crowley

52. What was the name of the gypsy and Tuscan Witch who helped Charles Leland write his book *Aradia, Gospel of the Witches?*
    a. Maddalena
    b. Esmarelda
    c. Morgana
    d. Tibuta

53. Who was the first to put forth the theory that the witches persecuted during the Inquisition were actually members of an organized Pagan religion, a fertility cult with roots that went back as far as Paleolithic times?
    a. Jules Michelet
    b. James Frazer
    c. Margaret Murray
    d. Gerald Gardner

54. In the countryside of modern-day Europe, you can see the remaining traces of agricultural folk customs, remnants of an ancient fertility cult that centered on the theme of the sacrificial grain king. Whose idea was this?
    a. Jules Michelet
    b. James Frazer
    c. Margaret Murray
    d. Doreen Valiente

55. He popularized the Pagan Celtic myth cycles in the British Isles through his writings about the White Goddess as muse and started the Celtic revival movement:
    a. James Frazer
    b. Joseph Campbell
    c. Robert Graves
    d. Alexei Kondratiev

56. Margaret Murray, noted archaeologist and Egyptologist, is best known for her theories on the origins of Witchcraft. She followed up her controversial 1921 book, *The Witch-*

cult in Western Europe, with another on the topic. It was titled
a. *The Witches' Bible*
b. *The God of the Witches*
c. *What Witches Do*
d. *Meaning of Witchcraft*

57. After the Witchcraft laws were repealed in England in 1951, he came forward to expound upon the ideas of Margaret Murray. He is credited with being the founder of the modern Witchcraft religion known as Wicca:
a. Alex Sanders
b. Gerald B. Gardner
c. Charles Leland
d. Robert Cochrane

58. What is the name of the coven Gerald Gardner said he had been initiated into in 1939?
a. Apple and Oak Coven
b. Hertfordshire Coven
c. Isis Reborn
d. New Forest Coven

59. What is the title of the first book published by Gerald Gardner?
a. *Witchcraft Today*
b. *High Magic's Aid*
c. *Kris and Other Malay Weapons*
d. *A Goddess Arrives*

60. Gardner became involved with a Co-Masonic occult group during the 1930s, members of which introduced him to Witchcraft and the Craft. They were called the
a. Co-Masons for Mary
b. First Rosicrucian Theater
c. Merry Wiccan Theater
d. Fellowship of Crotona

61. She is attributed with initiating and training Gerald Gardner in the ways of Witchcraft:
    a. Doreen Valiente
    b. Dorothy Clutterbuck
    c. Patricia Crowther
    d. Sybil Leek

62. In 1949, Gardner published his novel *High Magic's Aid*. What modern Wiccan concept was missing from it?
    a. the elements
    b. energy work
    c. spellwork
    d. the Goddess

63. Who wrote the introduction to Gardner's book *Witchcraft Today* (1954)?
    a. Doreen Valiente
    b. Margaret A. Murray
    c. James Frazer
    d. Robert Graves

64. He founded the Museum of Witchcraft in England:
    a. Cecil Williamson
    b. Gerald Gardner
    c. James Frazer
    d. Scott Cunningham

65. She was a well-known astrologer and psychic, both in England and in the United States. Her book *Diary of a Witch* was published in 1968, propelling her onto the media circuit, where she attempted to educate the public on Witchcraft:
    a. Patricia Crowther
    b. Sybil Leek
    c. Helen Duncan
    d. Dion Fortune

66. Later becoming a noted author in her own right, as Gerald Gardner's High Priestess she wrote and coauthored what

are considered some of the most beautiful rituals and inspirational poems in use today:

   a. Doreen Valiente

   b. Dion Fortune

   c. Patricia Crowther

   d. Sybil Leek

67. After Gardner's death in 1964, what happened to his Craft materials?

   a. destroyed, as is the proper way to dispose of a Witch's personal Book of Shadows

   b. sold to the Ripley's Believe It or Not! organization

   c. distributed to his closest friends

   d. given to the Farrars, who published them

68. Dion Fortune contributed to the modern Wiccan movement through a series of novels. Which of the following was not written by her?

   a. *The Sea Priestess*

   b. *The Demon Lover*

   c. *The Winged Bull*

   d. *The Heart of the Fire*

69. A controversial occultist during the twentieth century, he was a Ceremonial Magician whose writing and ideas had a major influence on the founders of the modern Witchcraft movement:

   a. Aleister Crowley

   b. Gerald Gardner

   c. Cecil Williamson

   d. Raymond Buckland

70. Helena Petrovna Blavatsky, a Russian spiritualist and clairvoyant, founded the Theosophical Society in 1875. This group was dedicated to

   a. the revival of the ancient Pagan religions

   b. bringing the word of the Goddess to Her people

   c. separating the occult from the mundane world of science

d. the joining of the Eastern and Western mystery traditions with modern science

71. Although the contemporary Witchcraft movement in the United States had been in existence prior to this event, many still mark it as the point that interest in Wicca and Paganism exploded:
    a. the first Pagan festival, held in Minneapolis in 1969
    b. Raymond Buckland's arrival in the United States
    c. The publication of *The Spiral Dance* and *Drawing Down the Moon*
    d. the accepted presence of Wiccans at the Parliament of World Religions

72. This was the first federally recognized Neo-Pagan religious organization:
    a. the Celtic Church
    b. the Covenant of the Goddess
    c. the Church of Wicca
    d. the Church of All Worlds

73. They founded the first recognized church of Wicca in the United States, giving religious credence to the words *Wicca* and *Witchcraft*:
    a. Tim Zell and Lance Christie
    b. Aidan Kelly and Alison
    c. Gavin and Yvonne Frost
    d. Janet and Stewart Farrar

74. Wicca was first upheld as a legitimate religion in a federal court of appeal in 1986. The question was raised in a case concerning
    a. prisoner's rights
    b. child custody
    c. employment termination
    d. site permit

75. He founded the Witches'Anti-Defamation League in New York City to help ensure Witches' religious rights and edu-

cate the public about Witchcraft. He also held the first "Witch-In" in Central Park:
a. Raymond Buckland
b. Isaac Bonewits
c. Leo Martello
d. Herman Slater

76. The Council of Witches was formed in 1973 for the purpose of
a. stopping the Witch Wars
b. defining the principles of Wicca
c. electing the "King" and "Queen" of the Witches
d. lobbying for Wicca as a religion

77. Initiated into the Faerie Tradition by Victor Anderson in the mid-1970s, she wrote of her experiences in a book still considered a primer for many practitioners of Wicca:
a. Macha NightMare
b. Starhawk
c. Mary Daly
d. Margot Adler

78. Author of *Positive Magic,* Marion Weinstein is sometimes referred to as "The Ethical Witch" for her stand on magic for beneficial purposes. For fourteen years, beginning in 1969, she was also well known for
a. her radio show
b. her flamboyant style of dress
c. her cable TV show on cooking with magic
d. her artwork featured in upscale magazines

79. The Witches League of Public Awareness (WLPA), an international educational organization, was organized in 1986 by renowned Salem Witch Laurie Cabot. It was originally created in response to
a. a child custody case
b. a prisoner's rights case
c. the local filming of a movie
d. the town not allowing her store in Salem

80. As owner of Llewellyn Worldwide, Ltd., one of the largest publishers of New Age books, he had a major influence on the early years of Wicca in the United States:
    a. Carl Weschke
    b. Herman Slater
    c. Raymond Buckland
    d. Tim Zell

81. An author and journalist, she was the first writer to document the emerging and growing Pagan religious movement in the United States:
    a. Margot Adler
    b. Starhawk
    c. Phyllis Curott
    d. Doreen Valiente

82. This group was founded at Carleton College in 1963 as a protest against the college's required religious service attendance. The popularity of their rituals was one of the impetuses for the revoking of the campus policy, yet they continued to meet, giving rise to one of the leading Pagan Druid organizations:
    a. Ár nDraíocht Féin
    b. New Druids of the U.S.
    c. Reformed Druids of North America
    d. White Willow

83. It began as a joke when these two authors, Ray Sherwin and Peter Carroll, published their book in the 1970s, but many believed that their theories hold the most likely explanation of how or why magic works. By 1986, Carroll formally began training people in
    a. Theosophy principles
    b. Schroeder's cat theory
    c. Illuminates of Thanateros
    d. space continuum practice

84. Incorporated on Samhain 1975, this church was founded in California by a group of Elders from a wide variety of Wic-

can Traditions. It has grown to have local councils throughout the United States, making it one of the oldest Wiccan
religious organizations:
a. Covenant of the Goddess
b. Church of All Worlds
c. the Wiccan Church
d. the Church of Bob

85. The creation of the New Reformed Orthodox Order of the
Golden Dawn (NROOGD) was inspired by
a. a vision of Crowley
b. A. E. Waite's secret notes
c. the results of a college assignment
d. a need to find another form of religious service that would
   include the consuming of alcohol

86. Laurie Cabot is known for the dramatic black robes and
pentacle jewelry that she always wears in public. In 1977,
she was given the title of
a. The Wickedest Witch in Massachusetts
b. President of the Witches League
c. Official Witch of Salem, Massachusetts
d. Cosmetics Spokesperson for Miss Clairol

87. Founded by Selena Fox and located on a two hundred-acre
nature preserve and herb farm in Wisconsin, this location
has become one of the best-known interfaith Pagan centers:
a. EarthSpirit Community
b. Circle Network
c. Circle Sanctuary
d. Cauldron Farm

88. He was one of the most prolific writers on the Craft, penning books on everything from *Magical Herbalism* (1982)
to *Crystal, Gem and Metal Magic* (1987). One of his best-
known titles was written for those people who wish to practice
on their own—*Wicca, A Guide for the Solitary Practitioner*
(1988):
a. Scott Cunningham

    b. Leo Martello

    c. Gavin Bone

    d. Raymond Buckland

89. This couple was initiated by Alex Sanders. They eventually formed their own covens in England and Ireland. Today, it's said that 75 percent of covens in Ireland can in some way trace their lineage back to them. They authored several books, but two of them—which were later combined into one—included many rituals and materials relating to the religion of the Craft:

    a. Gavin and Yvonne Frost

    b. Janet and Stewart Farrar

    c. Tzipora Katz and Kenny Klein

    d. Oberon and Morning Glory Zell

90. This noted author was raised in the New Forest area. She was initiated into the Craft by Alex Sanders at age eighteen. Later, she became involved with the Pagan Federation in England, becoming for a time its president. But it was her books on Wicca and Witchcraft that brought her name to the forefront of Pagan movement in both Europe and the United States:

    a. Vivianne Crowley

    b. Doreen Valiente

    c. Patricia Crowther

    d. Z. Budapest

91. Initiated into the Craft by Raymond and Rosemary Buckland, Ed Fitch is one of the primary founders and contributors to a more public format of the Craft. It is called

    a. the Wiccan Way

    b. the Pagan Way

    c. Pagan Gathering Force

    d. the Wiccan Circle Celebration

92. Our Pagan community has grown considerably since 1951. She cowrote a book with Starhawk reminding us that with the passage of time, we all will age and will someday face the

Crone. While we celebrate life, there is also need to embrace and honor all the cycles of Nature, including the endings:
a. Vivianne Crowley
b. Macha NightMare
c. Mary Daly
d. Judy Harrow

93. In 1993, when this event was held for the first time in a century, Witches and Pagans were granted not only representation but also active participation and acceptance as a religion:
a. the opening of Stonehenge to the public
b. the Parliament of World Religions
c. Harvard University's Gathering of Religions
d. the Folk and Mythology Festival

SECTION 6

Our Wiccan and Pagan Elders—Trivia Pursuit!

This may not be required knowledge, but it sure is fun! These are the tidbits of information that show just how human our Wiccan and Pagan Elders—those who were active in forming the modern Pagan movement—could really be.

94. Which noted Wiccan author was also a B-movie actress and model?
a. Judy Harrow
b. Laurie Cabot
c. Vivianne Crowley
d. Janet Farrar

95. Mixing magic with magick, this stage magician was a good friend of Gerald Gardner. He entertained the soon-to-be-queen Elizabeth at Buckingham Palace, along with the titled gentry of England:
a. Jeff McBride
b. Harry Houdini

    c. Arnold Crowther

    d. Cecil Williamson

96. Her grandfather, a renowned psychiatrist, probably would have thought she was crazy if he knew she became a High Priestess in the Craft:

    a. Margot Adler

    b. Starhawk

    c. Doreen Valiente

    d. Patricia Crowther

97. She went by the nickname Mimi throughout her childhood and into adulthood:

    a. Marion Weinstein

    b. Margot Adler

    c. Starhawk

    d. Silver RavenWolf

98. She was arrested in 1975 for giving a Tarot reading to an undercover police officer:

    a. Zsuzsanna (Z.) Budapest

    b. Starhawk

    c. Marion Weinstein

    d. Macha NightMare

99. He received a bachelor of arts in magic in 1970 from the University of California at Berkeley. His diploma was signed by Ronald Reagan, the acting governor of California:

    a. Aidan Kelly

    b. Scott Cunningham

    c. Leo Martello

    d. Isaac Bonewits

100. As a reporter for his local paper, he showed up to write a story about a strange group of Witches, and stayed. He was later initiated into the Craft by the gentleman he came to interview:

    a. Raymond Buckland

    b. Stewart Farrar

c. Arnold Crowther
d. Victor Anderson

101. Whose wedding ceremony was the first Wiccan handfasting to be written up in the society pages of *The New York Times*?
a. Laura A. Wildman and Thomas P. Hanlon
b. Phyllis Curott and Bruce Fields
c. Margot Adler and Dr. John Gliedman
d. Oberon and Morning Glory Zell

102. This poet earned his living working for the Internal Revenue Service and the Department of Health, Education and Welfare:
a. Issac Bonewits
b. Victor Anderson
c. Gwydion Pendderwen
d. Robert Graves

103. His knowledge of the occult came to the attention of the British government just prior to World War II. He was recruited to help the M16 intelligence section of the Foreign Office collect information about Nazi occult interests. He formed the Witchcraft Research Center for this purpose:
a. Gerald Gardner
b. Arnold Crowther
c. Stewart Farrar
d. Cecil Williamson

104. How did Doreen Valiente come to meet Gerald Gardner?
a. through a newspaper article
b. the Fellowship of Crotonia
c. a garden party at Dafo's
d. a meeting of the Folk Society

105. Dion Fortune is her magical name. Her mundane name was
a. Miriam Simos
b. Mary Lou Harris
c. Violet Mary Firth
d. Penny Novak

106. What does the *B* stand for in Gerald B. Gardner's name?
    a. Braun
    b. Brian
    c. Brosseau
    d. Brosco

107. What was Gerald Gardner's High Priestess's magical name?
    a. Lady Rhea
    b. Dafo
    c. Breida
    d. Cassandra

108. Under what name was Gardner's book *High Magic's Aid* (1949) published?
    a. Herne
    b. Jack Brown
    c. Scire
    d. Sybil

109. Z. Budapest founded her coven on the Winter Solstice in 1971. It was called
    a. the Compost Coven
    b. the Susan B. Anthony Coven
    c. the Coven of Uppity Women
    d. Diana's Dolls

110. Marion Weinstein is also known as
    a. an entertainer, doing stand-up comedy
    b. a stage magician
    c. a gourmet chef
    d. a character on *The Muppet Show*

111. What was the name of Starhawk's first coven?
    a. the Coven of Uppity Women
    b. Susan B. Anthony Coven
    c. Compost and Raving
    d. Fiery Females

112. She learned to drive by driving her dad's tractor at age eight

in South Jersey. In 1958, she was crowned Miss VFW Post 6295 in Burlington County:

a. Starhawk
b. Macha NightMare
c. Margot Adler
d. Marion Weinstein

113. This founder of one of the larger Pagan sects was legally blind. In 1957, he was tried twice in San Jose for "practicing Satanism," and was acquitted both times:

a. Leo Martello
b. Scott Cunningham
c. Alex Sanders
d. Victor Anderson

114. Ár nDraíocht Féin is Gaelic for

a. bet you can't pronounce this
b. our own Druidism
c. *Erin go bragh*
d. pass the whiskey

Answers to Chapter 3

Unless otherwise stated, give yourself *2 points for each correct answer.* At the end of the chapter, add together your totals from each section to get your final score for the chapter. This number will be carried forward to the end of the book for a final tally!

SECTION 1
Witchcraft in the Ages

1. A. Our nomadic ancestors practiced a form of tribal Shamanism. These Priests and Priestesses acted as mediators between the spirit world and the community. They would find and call the herds for the hunters, interpret the natural signs around them, and communicate with the spirits of ancestors.

2. D. The Oracle of Delphi was consulted by individuals, ambassadors, generals, and statesmen from cities all over the Greek world. At this point in the historical time line, we see the clear split between two types of magic workers: first, the Priests and Priestesses of the temple, and second, the witches or sorcerers who worked on the local folk level. The first is organized religion and the second a profession or trade, like carpentry or breadmaking.

3. C. Apuleius was the author of *The Golden Ass,* written in the second century C.E. It contains some of the earliest stories about Witches. Unfortunately, they are not placed in a very positive light. Apuleius parodies the two types of magic users, Priests and Witches, portraying them as either superstitious ninnies or lying charlatans.

4. C. This passage, found in Exodus 22: 18, was the justification used to put to death people identified as Witches during the Inquisition. The actual word used in the Hebrew Bible is *m'khashephah,* and it does translate to a form of magic worker. The Hebrews, along with members of almost every other culture, acknowledged a distinct difference between those they might describe as working magic for good (what today we would call scientists or doctors) and those who did malicious harm, the taking of life or destroying property through psychic means. These malevolent people would "cast" their spells in private and from a distance, leaving no evidence of their crime. This secret and hidden evil

nature of the *m'khashephah*, is what the biblical writers were afraid of and the practice they wanted to root out and eliminate. The major change that occurred much later during the Inquisition was the combining of all those who worked magic under the same heading, witch.

5. D. Certain European folklore included the existence of night spirits. Similar to vampirism, these nocturnal spirits (usually women) drank the blood of their human victims. The sentence for those charged with such nighttime activity was death. The new Christian faith scoffed at the idea of cannibal spirits and encouraged the Christian kings to forbid the lynching of women accused of this practice. This actually led to a decline in the number of people killed as witches.

6. D. The Canon Episcopi was one of the most important ecclesiastical documents of the Middle Ages. Recorded in 900 C.E., it defined Witchcraft as devil worship but also declared it to be nothing more than foolish delusion.

   For Your Learning Enjoyment: The Nicene Creed is the statement of Christian beliefs, put together at the Council of Nicaea in 325 C.E. The Reformation occurred in the 1530s. This schism of Protestant doctrine from the Catholic faith created a spiritual mess in Europe. The Papal Reform Movement of 1049 through 1054 was the reshaping of the priesthood. The reform took away privileges from priests, such as marriage and the benefits that go with that estate.

7. B. Thomas Aquinas (1226–1274), a noted author and theologian of his day, believed in the devil as an actual being and that all heretics were, by nature, involved with the devil whether or not they realized it. Translated, it meant that if you did not follow the church, you were a heretic—hence a devil worshiper and a sorcerer or witch. Aquinas's teachings are completely contrary to the Canon Episcopi, which acknowledged the existence of devil worship, but called it foolishness. He also eliminated the distinction between "good" and "malevolent" magic, placing them both in the

devil-worshiping category. His suggested means of dealing with heretics was death by burning. Lovely fellow, wasn't he?

For Your Learning Enjoyment: Pope Leo IX gave the order for the Papal Reform in 1049 through 1054 that doomed priests to celibacy. Tomás de Torquemada was the notorious Grand Inquisitor in Spain in 1483. Pope Urban II set in motion the First Crusade in 1095.

8. A. While the witch trials and executions were occurring around him, Reginald Scot was one of the loudest among those who stood against the persecution of witches and the popular beliefs about witchcraft. In his opinion, there were four categories of witches: those falsely accused; those who were mentally unstable and delusional; evil witches who caused harm through natural means but did not really have powers; and imposters who preyed on the ignorant. His opinions, which did have some influence on the clergy of England, so angered King James I that he responded with a book of his own titled *Daemonologie*.

9. D. Agrippa's full name was Henty Cornelius Agrippa von Nettesheim (1486–1535). How would you like to write that every time you signed your name! Agrippa's *On Occult Philosophy* was a summation of all the magical and occult knowledge of the time. It had a profound influence on practitioners of the occult and the development of Western occult thought. He argued that what was called magic was actually a natural psychic gift and had nothing to do with the devil. He believed that the connection between will and imagination can effect magic, and in the power of mind over body. He also believed that the highest potential for magic could be found within the harmony of Nature.

10. A. Read Michelet and you might think, based on the theories presented, that you're reading a modern book on Wicca. He argues that Witchcraft was actually the survival of an older fertility cult that had been repressed by the

Catholic Church. Michelet's writings had an effect on God-frey Leland, Margaret Murray, and Gerald Gardner, the progenitors of the modern Wiccan movement.

11. C. The Hellfire Club was opened by Sir Francis Dashwood in the eighteenth century. Members dressed as monks or fri-ars and ate, drank, gambled, and indulged in sexual esca-pades. Although a parody of devil worship may have been enacted, members were not actually Satanists or witches. Their last meeting was in 1762 . . . although I think I've seen members, or at least the spirit of the club, at a number of Pagan festivals. The reason that the appearance, and the pop-ularity, of this club is important is that it shows how quickly and far the opinions of the populace had moved from those expressed during the Inquisition—from fear to parody.

12. A. *Cunning person* is a medieval term loosely associated with white Witches (as compared with evil Witches). They worked popular folk magic, herbalism, divination, and counter-spells.
    For Your Learning Enjoyment: Hedge Witch is a new term coined by English Witch Rae Beth and is a modern view of the cunning person. A Hedge Witch differs from the older counterpart in that a cunning person would have been illit-erate, most likely did not worship the God and Goddess, and would not have limited work to just "good" magic. *Peller* is a Cornish/Celtic word that literally means "dis-tancer." It is someone skilled at breaking or "driving away" hexes and in divining, especially for lost items.

TOTAL YOUR POINTS
Chapter 3, section 1: Witchcraft in the Ages

_____ Total number of questions 1–12 answered correctly

Multiply the total number of questions 1–12 answered correctly by 2. This will give you your total number of points for chapter 3, section 1:

_____ X 2 = _____
Total number of questions   Total score, chapter 3,
1–12 answered correctly   section 1

Total possible points for chapter 3, section 1 = 24

SECTION 2

You Have the Right to Remain Silent—
Witchcraft and the Law

13. C. The earliest known Roman legal codes contained
     edicts to punish people who cast baneful spells. Punish-
     ment could include the death penalty if magic was used to
     hurt or kill someone, or damage property. There is a dis-
     tinct difference between what we would call Witchcraft
     and the way the term was used in ancient history or even in
     other cultures. For example, those who worked divination
     or were herbalists are what we today would call scientists
     or doctors. The beliefs that there are those who work in se-
     cret to hurt others, and that they deserve punishment, are
     universal. This is also the type of "witch" referred to in the
     Hebrew Bible.

14. C. Henry VIII in 1542. This law allowed witches to be
     tried and punished by the state instead of just by the
     church. It made it a felony to be involved with magical acts
     of malevolence. Love magic, which they termed "unlawful
     love," was deemed a crime worthy of capital punishment. It
     was repealed by Henry's son, Edward VI, in 1547 but was
     reestablished, through ecclesiastical pressure, in 1563 by Eliza-
     beth I.

15. D. King James I (of England), James VI (of Scotland). The
     act was passed by Parliament with the approval of King
     James. James had developed a personal vendetta against
     witches after hearing that a coven, the North Berwich

Witches, claimed to have tried to sink his ship by using weather magic as he traveled from Denmark. James added to the hysteria over witches when he authored *Daemonologie* (1597), a book on the malicious and evil nature of witches. He seemed to mellow and become more cynical with age. He pardoned several accused witches because of lack of solid evidence and even exposed a few fraudulent accusations.

16. C. Under the old Elizabethan code, put into place by Queen Elizabeth in 1547, if you were found guilty of malicious magic use and it was your first offense, the punishment would be one year in jail and pillory time. A second offense was punishable by death. Those who practiced baneful love magic or treasure seeking were sentenced to life in prison. The Witchcraft Act of 1604 in England issued death on the first offense of harm by witchcraft and for any conjuring of evil spirits—although invoking benign spirits was okay. It was not repealed until 1736, when it was replaced by a new law.

17. A. The 1604 Witchcraft Act was repealed by George II of England. It was replaced with a new statute that included prosecution of those who pretended to possess magical powers such as witchcraft, enchantment, divination, or the conjuring of spirits. The punishment dropped from the death penalty to one year in jail and time in the stocks.

18. C. Helen Duncan, a known medium, was not the last person sentenced in England under the 1736 Witchcraft Act, but she is often listed as being such. In actuality, the law had already been removed from the books. Duncan was imprisoned for nine months in 1944 on charges of having violated the security laws when she channeled the spirit of a drowned sailor who had been on one of His Majesty's ships. She did this before it was made public that the ship had been lost.

19. C. Through the hard work of Spiritualists, 1736 witchcraft laws were repealed in 1951 and replaced with the Fraudu-

lent Mediums Act. For the first time since 1542, Witchcraft was not illegal, and Witches and Pagans were free to practice their religion.

20. D. While some individual states still have laws again spiritualism and fortune-telling, there has never been a federal law against witchcraft.

 TOTAL YOUR POINTS
Chapter 3, section 2: Witchcraft and the Law

_____ Total number of questions 13–20 answered correctly

Multiply the total number of questions 13–20 answered correctly by 2. This will give you your total number of points for chapter 3, section 2:

_____ X 2 = _____
Total number of questions   Total score, chapter 3,
13–20 answered correctly   section 2

Total possible points for chapter 3, section 2 = 16

SECTION 3

The Blood of the Ancients— The Burning Times

21. C. The Burning Times refers to the period of intense witch hunting and executions that occurred in Europe and the Americas. Rumbles started in the fourteenth century on the heels of the Black Plague (1347–1359). During that time, the rumor was spread that the plague was a form of chemical warfare facilitated by those against the church—namely Jews, Muslims, and witches. At this point, we begin to see an increase in trials, with the first mass trials and executions of witches occurring in the fifteenth century.

22. A. According to Jenny Gibbons, historian, the mass hysteria largely occurred from 1550 to 1650, during the height of the religious strife caused by the schism between the Catholic and Protestant Churches otherwise known as the Reformation. This was followed by sharp decline after 1650 and the eventual disappearance of witch persecutions in the eighteenth century.

23. B. The localized secular courts—the courts that were made up of those within the accused's community—killed up to 90 percent of those brought before them accused of witchcraft. The national secular, or king's courts, condemned about 30 percent of those accused. According to current research, the rate of those brought before the church and accused of witchcraft who were given the death penalty was extremely low. The purpose of the church Inquisition was to bring the souls of heretics back to the church. The church courts tended to grant lenient penalties, and the Inquisition pardoned many who confessed and repented. In fact, the Spanish Inquisition worked hard to keep witch trials out of the civil courts. While they held control, no witches were condemned. When the secular court regained power, three hundred people were executed before the Inquisition managed to stop the trials. You had a better chance surviving with the church than with your next-door neighbor on the jury!

24. C. The inquisition—with a small *i*—comes from the word *inquire*. It is a type of civil trial used throughout Europe. The Inquisition—capital *I*—was a branch of the church ordered to stamp out heresy. This is where a lot of confusion has come up for historians doing research on the European witch trials. The *i* versus *I* has caused many scholars to take another look at their original conclusions.

25. C. Contrary to popular belief, the Inquisition was not created to persecute witches. The original goal of the Inquisition was to weed out Christian heresy and the enemies of

the church. Their first targets were other Christian sects, such as the Cathars, whose popularity had so grown that they had spread over much of Europe. The association of witches with heresy came later.

26. A. Heresy is any deviation from the orthodox teachings of the church. To the Catholic Church, a Protestant, a Jew, and a Witch would all be considered heretics, along with members of any other Christian or non-Christian sect.

27. A. Innocent IV expanded prohibitions against heresy and encouraged enforcement by granting permission for the secular authorities to use torture, imprisonment, and execution on behalf of the church and, once guilt was established, permission to confiscate the personal possessions of heretics. In essence, he created a new paying profession.

28. B. Pope Innocent VIII is credited with launching the Inquisition of witches, but in actuality he was merely building upon previous bulls against heresy and sorcery. The new bull included a strict ruling that allowed the Inquisition full authority to do whatever was needed to carry out its inquisitions and demanded that the local authorities aid them in their work. The witch finders, armed with their copies of the soon-to-be-released *Malleus Maleficarum*—"torture for dummies"—started their hunts.

29. A. The Dominicans, also called the "Order of Friars Preachers," were given that honor by Pope Gregory IX in 1233. In addition, they were answerable only to the pope. The Franciscans, Carmelites, and Augustinians are other orders of friars, but they didn't make the cut.

30. B. The Witches' Hammer or the Hammer Against Witchcraft. Based on the biblical passage "thou shalt not suffer a witch to live" (Exodus 22: 18), it is a manual for the identification, torture, and prosecution of witches.

31. D. It was a top seller, second only to the Bible until 1678. There were sixteen editions by 1669, and it is still being

published today, although now it is used for anthropological, theological, and historical study instead of as a factual book on the identification and sentencing of witches. Check any online bookseller, and you can purchase a copy in paperback or hardcover.

32. A. Heinrich Kramer and Jakob Sprenger. Kramer and Sprenger were both Dominican monks. Kramer was the primary author of the *Malleus*. After the success of the book, he was appointed Inquisitor for the provinces of Tyrol, Bohemia, Salzburg, and Moravia. Kramer was eventually tossed out of the order for various infractions. Sprenger, on the other hand, did well for himself. He was named prior and regent of studies at the Cologne Convent.

33. D. The split between the Protestant and Catholic Churches—the Reformation—of 1550 C.E. caused shock waves that shook communities both spiritually and politically. With neighbor against neighbor, it isn't surprising that many tried to find something to focus their attentions on and pin their problems to. The witch trials were at their height when both the church and the state were torn by religious strife and weakness. In contrast, when the state, the church, or both were strong, then the numbers of witch trials were low.

34. D. Matthew Hopkins (?–1647?), the self-dubbed "Witch-finder General," is what could only be described as an evil man. Known to have condemned at least 230 people, he employed methods of torture, lies, and deceit to get his targets to the gallows. A witch finder for profit, he would sell his services, at a high price, to towns. His method was to listen to gossip until he routed out someone in the community who wasn't spoken of highly or who was already suspected of witchcraft. He would then use torture and deceit to extract a confusion. He was very successful at his trade and was in much demand for a time. Eventually, he was criticized for his greed and excessive force, and judges began to turn on him. He disappeared in 1647.

35. B. Christians. Most people died with a "Hail Mary" or the Lord's Prayer on their lips. Very, very few people were actual witches. Those who died were victims of hysteria, greed, or general dislike by their community. Ironically enough, the vast majority of those who could be called "white" witches—the healers and midwives—were never accused. These people and their services were a necessary part of the community.

36. D. There are some known cases in which a doctor, unable to cure his patient, accused a local healer of witchcraft, but this did not happen very often. Unhappy patients and other healers trying to gain more business were often the ones who pointed fingers and cried, "Witch!"

37. A. Based on recent scholarship, which includes Pagan historians, the numbers often quoted for total deaths during the Burning Times are way off. To date, it looks like between fifty and sixty thousand died, but that number may go lower as trials are confirmed.

38. B. In most areas, women carried the brunt of the witchcraft accusations—with the exception of Scandinavia, which was an equal-death-opportunity country, and Iceland, where the majority of those accused were men. At twenty-six thousand, Central Europe holds the record for the highest number of condemned, most of whom were women.

39. D. The Spanish Inquisition was very skeptical of the evil presence of witchcraft in the community. Claiming that only they had the right to condemn witches—which they refused to do—they removed witch trials from the civil into the church courts. In 1616, however, the secular authorities again gained control. They executed three hundred people before the Spanish Inquisition was able to stop the trials. On the other hand, if you were Jewish you were considered a heretic, a crime punishable by death. There would be very little chance of escaping the flames.

40. A. At twenty-six thousand, Germany ranks the highest in the death toll. Scotland also ranks up there with around two thousand. It is interesting to note that Germany and Switzerland (which also had more than its fair share of witch-trial-related deaths) are also two countries that were made up of dozens of small, loosely put together, independent states. In addition, they both experienced a high degree of religious strife during the Reformation.

41. C. Ireland is recorded as having only eight witch trials, and of those only four witches were condemned.

 TOTAL YOUR POINTS
Chapter 3, section 3: The Burning Times

_____   Total number of questions 21–41 answered correctly

Multiply the total number of questions 21–41 answered correctly by 2. This will give you your total number of points for chapter 3, section 2:

_____ X 2 = _____
Total number of questions   Total score, chapter 3,
21–41 answered correctly   section 3

Total possible points for chapter 3, section 3 = 42

SECTION 4

Witchcraft Is a Hanging Offense— The Witch Hysteria in the U.S.

42. A. Danvers (aka Salem village), not Salem, Massachusetts. There were never any witchcraft accusations in Salem. Although nearby and loosely associated, Salem village was separate from the town of Salem. They had different churches and different communities. Sometime after the trials, the name of Salem village was changed to Danvers . . . but don't

tell Laurie Cabot, the "official Witch of Salem," or all the tourists who come to share in the Witch experience that they're in the wrong village!

43. A.   The Reverend Parris brought with him to Salem village Tituba and her husband, John. Tituba cared for the reverend's daughter, Betty, and his niece, Abigail Williams. She most likely kept the girls entertained with stories from her homeland, Barbados, and possibly told them about some of the native Vodoun practices. They told their friends, and soon all the girls began playing with forms of divination to find out information about their possible future husbands. Shortly afterward, some of the girls began having demonic visions and fits. Ironically, Tituba was probably the only one accused of witchcraft who had some actual knowledge of the craft. When accused, she confessed to being a witch and was put in jail. There she remained while the hysteria continued outside until she was acquitted and released in May 1693. She was then sold as a slave to cover her court costs.

44. B.   It is said that Sarah Good's husband was not a good provider. She was, however, a strong women who took care of herself and, if need be, would take to begging to survive. Sarah Osborne was old and bedridden. She had made the mistake some years back of living with her husband prior to marriage. Tituba was also one of the first accused. All of these women were independent, and outcasts in their community. None was a member of the church. Old and frail, Sarah Osborne died in jail shortly after her imprisonment.

45. C.   Spectral evidence—the visions and performances of the girls who claimed to see the spirits who were tormenting them—was the only evidence put forth in trial.

46. A.   Bridget Bishop was hung on June 10, 1692. She had been known to entertain frequently in her home, wore red dresses, and drank liquor. Because of her flamboyant lifestyle, many were willing to believe she was a witch even be-

fore she was accused. The witch trials escalated after her death.

For Your Learning Enjoyment: Elizabeth Proctor was granted a stay of execution because she was pregnant. The delay saved her life. She was later acquitted and released. Rebecca Nurse was originally acquitted, but the girls forced the jury to reconsider. This time they found her guilty. She was so beloved by her friends that they wrote a petition to Governor Phips asking him to reprieve her, but she was executed on July 19, 1692. George Burroughs was hung on August 19, 1692. He shocked the crowd by perfectly reciting the Lord's Prayer, something a witch was not supposed to be able to do. Over the outcries of the audience, Cotton Mather gave the order to finish the execution despite this sign of possible innocence.

47. B. Cotton Mather, a Puritan minister in Boston, wrote *Memorable Providences Relating to Witchcraft* (1689) and *Wonders of the Invisible World* (1693). He firmly believed in witchcraft, yet was skeptical about spectral evidence. Mather tried to convince the judges to use other methods to prosecute the witches.

For Your Learning Enjoyment: It was an ancestor of Nathaniel Hawthorne, not Hawthorne himself, who was involved with the trials. Justice Stoughton was the chief justice of the trials. He firmly believed that the devil could not control an innocent child and held that spectral evidence must be true. The Reverend Noyes was a witch hunter who was there from the beginning of the trials. He was cursed by Sarah Good when he pressed her to confess. She is quoted as saying, "I am no more a witch than you are a wizard, and if you take away my life, God will give you blood to drink." He supposedly died years later of a hemorrhage that caused him to choke on his own blood.

48. C. Giles Corey was a wealthy landowner. His wife, Martha Giles, was accused of witchcraft before him. Giles at first thought she was guilty and begged Martha to confess

(which she refused to do). After her pronouncement of guilt, fingers were pointed at him. Realizing that if he confessed to being a witch, or if he was found guilty of witchcraft, his property would be confiscated and his children would not inherit any of his holdings, Giles refused to acknowledge the court's right to try him. He was tortured by having a board placed across his chest and with heavy stones placed upon it. As the weight slowly crushed him alive, he was begged to confess. The proud man just replied, "More weight." He died without a confession. His wife was hung days later, but his children inherited his estate.

49. C. There were 50 accusers (that is, 50 people who claimed to see specters and witches) over 160 people accused, 31 condemned, and 19 executed. One person died under torture, and at least 13 died in prison during the Salem witch trials of 1692 and 1693. The ages of those accused ranged from four to eighty years old.

50. A. The girls, drunk on their own power, accused Lady Phips, the wife of the royal governor. That was the last straw. The governor moved the court proceedings out of the village and disallowed any spectral evidence. Without the spectral evidence, there was no proof. Most of those being held were acquitted. Those condemned were granted reprieves. By May 9, 1693, it was over.

For Your Learning Enjoyment: The town of Andover requested that a few of the girls come to their town and root out any devil worship. The girls accused a number of folks until they pointed a finger at a wealthy gentleman from Boston. He responded by suing them for slander. The girls dropped the charges and quickly left town.

TOTAL YOUR POINTS
Chapter 3, section 4: The Witch Hysteria in the U.S.

_____   Total number of questions 42–50 answered correctly

Multiply the total number of questions 42–50 answered correctly
by 2. This will give you your total number of points for chapter 3,
section 4:

_____ X 2 = _____
Total number of questions   Total score, chapter 3,
42–50 answered correctly   section 4

Total possible points for chapter 3, section 4 = 18

SECTION 5

Give Me That Old-Time Religion—
The Modern Magical Movement

51. A. Charles G. Leland (1824–1903) published his book
Aradia, Gospel of the Witches in 1890. He attempted to
prove the existence of a religion based upon witchcraft that
stretches back into antiquity. The book contains spells, stories, and a statement from the Goddess Diana to her daughter Aradia. This address included lines that were later
incorporated into the modern version of the Charge of the
Goddess.

52. A. *Aradia* was written with the help of a Italian peasant
woman who claimed to be a Florentine hereditary Witch.
She was referred to only as "Maddalena." Maddalena was
helping Leland collect folklore information. In 1866, she
told him of the existence of a manuscript that detailed the
old Pagan religion, the so-called Aradia, or the Gospel of the
Witches. She never provided him with the original, but gave
him handmade copies of the document.

53. C. Margaret Alice Murray (1863–1963) was a noted archaeologist and Egyptologist when she produced her controversial theories about the origins of Witchcraft in Europe
in her book *The Witch-cult in Western Europe* (1921). Her
theory was that the Christian heresy found throughout

Europe during the Inquisitions was actually the remnant of an older, organized Pagan fertility religion that had been practiced continually since Paleolithic times. Much of her research has been discredited by others in her field, although her theories inspired many, including Gerald Gardner. Michelet, in his work *La Sorciere,* had a similar notion, but his theory was that the people persecuted were practicing the last surviving remains of a pre-Christian fertility religion, the organization of which was long gone. Frazer is yet another who had a similar idea, which you'll find in the answer to the next question.

54. B. Sir James George Frazer published his work *The Golden Bough: A Study in Magic and Religion* in 1890. Basing his ideas on the compilation of various mythologies, he concluded that the theme of the sacrificial agricultural grain king was, in Western culture, universal. Even the Christian religion was originally based on the model of the sacrificial king who willingly dies for the continued betterment of his people, and is later reborn. He concluded that the remnants of this ancient Pagan fertility cult could be seen in the agricultural folk traditions still practiced in the countryside. The origins of Witchcraft rituals and beliefs would also have been leftover bits of this cult.

55. C. Robert Graves published his work *The White Goddess* in 1946. Originally titled "The Roebuck in the Thicket," the book's theory is that ancient poetic myths served as the keepers of an ancient formula that makes up the components of a Celtic mystery religion. Joseph Campbell was a noted author on world mythology. Alexei Kondratiev is the author of *Celtic Rituals: An Authentic Guide to Ancient Celtic Spirituality* (1998).

56. B. Margaret Murray's second book was *The God of the Witches.* Published in 1931, it was her theory that the Satan whom people admitted to worshiping during the Inquisition was in reality the older horned fertility God of the

witches. According to Murray, this fertility religion, which could be traced back to Paleolithic times, never really died out but instead went underground. Modern scholars have rejected her theory for lack of evidence.

57. B. Gerald Gardner was a British civil servant in the 1920s and 1930s and worked in the Far East. After retirement, he spent much time traveling to various archaeological sites around Europe and Asia. Once back in England, he became friends with members of a group called the Fellowship of Crotona. They introduced him to their coven and the Craft.

58. D. The New Forest Coven was said to have existed in the New Forest area of Britain. Based in Hampshire, it is also sometimes referred to as the Southern Coven of British Witches. Gardner claimed that it was a genuine coven in the model that Murray had hypothesized, with ancient roots of continued existence.

59. C. *Kris and Other Malay Weapons,* Gardner's first book, was published in Singapore in 1939 and reprinted in England in 1973. The book is about the wavy-bladed ritual dagger and other ritual knives used within Malaysian religious and magical practices.

60. D. If you said B, however, you're technically correct. The Fellowship of Crotona was founded in 1911 in the New Forest, Hampshire, area. This Co-Mason group established "the First Rosicrucian Theater in England," which put on plays with occult themes. It was theater members within the fellowship who first introduced Gardner to the Craft.

61. B. Although recent scholarship has brought this into question, Dorothy Clutterbuck is still credited with having initiated Gerald Gardner into her New Forest Coven. It is possible that Gardner used the name *Clutterbuck* as a way to protect his actual priestess, known only as Dafo, whom he was involved with in the Co-Masonic Rosicrucian Theater.

62. D. Yup, the Goddess! While Gardner said his coven wor-

shiped the Goddess, his novel centers on the worship of "the old gods," never mentioning the Lady.

63. B.   Margaret Murray wrote the introduction to a book she believed supported her theories on the existence of an organized ancient fertility religion consistently practiced since Paleolithic times.

64. A.   Containing everything from Aleister Crowley's sword to poppets and talismans, the Museum of Witchcraft contains the largest collection of folk and modern magical artifacts in the world. It is located in Boscastle, Cornwall, England. After being run out of a site by the townspeople at Stratford-upon-Avon, Williamson located his museum in Castletown on the Isle of Man. It opened in 1949, with Gerald Gardner as the resident Witch. Gardner purchased the building but not its contents in 1952. He then filled the building with his own materials. After Williamson sold the building, he moved his collection to England. There, because towns rejected the idea of hosting a Witch museum, it bounced around to various locations until settling in Boscastle in 1960. Williamson continued to research the occult throughout his life, retiring and selling the museum in 1996. It is still in Boscastle and open to the public. My husband and I stumbled upon the Museum of Witchcraft during our honeymoon in 2000 and were thrilled to see that it still maintains an honest portrayal of Witchcraft and the development of modern Wicca.

65. B.   Sybil Leek claimed to be a hereditary Witch with a line that stretched back to 1134. In the 1960s, she immigrated to the United States, where she worked as an astrologer. *Diary of a Witch* was published in 1968. It was the first of sixty books that she published. She became popular on the media circuit, where she used her time to try to educate the public and dispel the myths about Witchcraft.

For Further Reading: Diary of a Witch by Sybil Leek. (NAL Signet Library, 1968).

66. A. Doreen Valiente is said to have contributed some of the most beautiful and influential pieces within the Craft. Her Charge of the Goddess, a reworking of materials found within Leland's *Aradia* and Crowley's writings, is considered a cornerstone of Wiccan belief. She is also the author of numerous books about Witchcraft, including *Natural Magic* (1975), *An ABC of Witchcraft Past and Present* (1973; 1984; 1986), and *Witchcraft for Tomorrow* (1978; 1983; 1985). Her autobiography is *The Rebirth of Witchcraft* (1989).

67. B. Lady Olwen was Gardner's last High Priestess. He willed to her his museum on the Isle of Man along with the bulk of his magical tools. Her young daughter was placed under supervisory probation for three years after an article appeared in papers accusing her of allowing her daughter to participate in Witch rites. When the probation ended, she sold the museum, including Gardner's materials, to the Ripley organization and immigrated to Spain.

    For More Information: The Triumph of the Moon by Ronald Hutton. (Oxford University Press, 1999).

68. D. Dion Fortune (1891–1946) was an adept in Ceremonial Magic and a prolific writer. Her novels with occult themes influenced, and still are popular among, modern Witches. They include *The Sea Priestess* (1938), *The Demon Lover* (1957), and *The Winged Bull* (1935). In addition, she has published numerous nonfiction books, including *Psychic Self-Defense* (1930) and *The Mystical Qabalah* (1936). *The Heart of the Fire* was written by Cerridwen Fallingstar, Cauldron Publications, 1990.

69. A. Crowley (1875–1947) was a Ceremonial Magician who also had a major impact on what was to become the modern movement of Wicca. Crowley enjoyed the "bad boy of magic" image given to him by the press. He was involved with the Hermetic Order of Golden Dawn and later the Ordo Templi Orientis (O.T.O.). One of his books, *The Book*

of the Law, includes the Law of Thelema, which is said by some to be the basis of the Wiccan Rede.

For Further Reading: Portable Darkness: An Aleister Crowley Reader, edited by Scott Michaelson. (Harmony Books, 1989). *The Legend of Aleister Crowley* by P. R. Stephenson and Israel Regardie (Llewellyn Publications, 1970).

70. D. Helena Petrovna Blavatsky (1831–1891) founded the Theosophical Society with Colonel H. S. Olcott in New York in 1875. The society was dedicated to the melding of the supernatural with natural science. She influenced the Ceremonial Magical realms, which, in turn, affected modern magical movements such as Wicca.

71. C. Publication of *The Spiral Dance* and *Drawing Down the Moon.*

72. D. The Church of All Worlds (CAW) was formally chartered on March 4, 1968, making it the first Pagan religion in the United States to be federally recognized. CAW was originally founded by Tim Zell and Lance Christie, students at Westminster College in St. Louis, in 1962.

73. C. Founded by Gavin and Yvonne Frost in 1968, the Church of Wicca achieved federal recognition by receiving IRS tax-exempt status as a religious organization in 1972, making it the first recognized church of Witchcraft in the United States. The School of Wicca is the Church's correspondence course segment.

74. A. In the prisoner's rights case of *Dettmer v. Landon* in 1986, the court of appeals for Virginia upheld a prior ruling acknowledging the Church of Wicca as a religion.

75. C. Leo Martello (d. 2000), a hereditary Sicilian Witch, activist for civil and gay rights, and author, began his notoriety in the 1960s when he went public as a Witch. He published his first book, *Weird Ways of Witchcraft,* in 1969. In 1970, he organized the first "Witch-In," in Central Park. Leo needed to secure the services of the ACLU in order to ob-

tain a permit for the event. This sparked the creation of the Witches Anti-Defamation League, of which branches have been formed throughout the United States.

76. B.   The Council of American Witches, an alliance of contemporary Witches from a variety of different traditions, was formed and active from 1973 to 1974. Its purpose was to define the principles of Wicca. These Principles of Wiccan Belief continue to be held by many as embracing the central core of beliefs held in modern Wicca. It has even been included in the handbook for the chaplains in the U.S. Army. The council disbanded after the creation of the document.

77. B.   Starhawk is a feminist and activist whose book *The Spiral Dance* is credited as one of the major influences in the modern Pagan movement in America. Her book blends feminist principles and politics into modern Witchcraft.

78. A.   Marion Weinstein began her radio career in 1969 at WBAI-FM. Known as *Marion's Cauldron,* it aired regularly for fourteen years. Weinstein conducted interviews, taught occult topics, and discussed psychic phenomena and Witchcraft.

79. C.   The Witches League of Public Awareness started as a protest against the filming of John Updike's novel *The Witches of Eastwick.* The book is about three Witches who become involved with the devil. WLPA does not handle individual discrimination cases, but is an organization for distributing information and to monitor the media in its treatment of Witches.

80. A.   Carl Weschke purchased Llewellyn Publishing Company in the 1960s. Moving it to Minneapolis in 1970, he opened the Gnostica Bookstore. He was influential in holding several annual festivals that helped bring Witches and Pagans from around the United States together. Weschke was also involved with the Council of American Witches. The Llewellyn Company is still one of the largest publishers of occult books.

81. A. *Drawing Down the Moon* was published on the same day as Starhawk's *The Spiral Dance*. While *The Spiral Dance* is a book on Wiccan ritual and practices, Margot Adler's *Drawing Down the Moon* takes a look at the diverse community already present at that time in the United States. It is based on interviews with more than a hundred people and groups, documenting their practices and beliefs.

82. C. The Reformed Druids of North America might have begun as a joke, but it quickly became a popular movement that extended well beyond Carleton College to groves throughout the United States.

83. C. The Order of Chaos Magic, called Illuminates of Thanateros, began as a joke, but by 1986 they were training people to be Magicians in their system.

84. A. The Covenant of the Goddess (CoG) incorporated on Samhain 1975, founded by Elders from diverse Wiccan traditions "to increase cooperation among Witches and to secure for Witches and covens the legal protection enjoyed by members of other religions." It is one of the largest and oldest Wiccan religious organizations and has the power to confer credentials upon clergy. CoG was one of the opponents of the Helms amendment when it was submitted in 1985. This amendment would have disallowed Wiccan and Pagan churches and organizations from religious tax-exempt status. Thanks to a massive letter-writing campaign and help from the ACLU, the amendment did not pass.

85. C. This was another one of those college assignments that proved more productive than the instructor, or the founders, could ever have imagined.

86. C. In 1977, then-governor Michael Dukakis gave Cabot her title of "the Official Witch of Salem." Outspoken and flamboyant, Laurie blew open her broom closet in the 1960s when she made the decision to live full time as a Witch and wear nothing but the black, flowing robes of a

Witch. In 1986, she established the Witches League for Public Awareness. She is the author of many books, including: *Practical Magic: A Salem Witch's Handbook* (1986), and *The Power of the Witch,* written with Tom Cowan (1990).

87. C. The Circle Network, founded in 1978 by Selena Fox, consists of organizations and individuals in more than fifty countries. Their guide to Pagan resources has been published continuously since 1979. In 1983, the church used its own funds to purchase Circle Sanctuary in Madison, Wisconsin. When local residents challenged the existence of Circle Sanctuary in 1984, with the assistance of the ACLU, Circle became the first Pagan organization to achieve recognition on the state level at a public hearing. Circle Sanctuary has sponsored a yearly national Pagan Spirit Gathering since 1981.

    For Your Learning Enjoyment: The EarthSpirit Community is located in Massachusetts. They put on numerous public Sabbat celebrations and have offered Pagan festivals since the early 1980s.

88. A. Scott Cunningham (1956–1993) was a prolific Wiccan author, penning more than thirty fiction and nonfiction books before his death in 1993.

89. B. Janet and Stewart are well known on both sides of the pond. Their books *Eight Sabbats for Witches* (1981) and *The Witches' Way* (1984) were combined and published in the United States as *The Witches' Bible* (1984). They have been used by many as a guideline for forming a coven.

90. A. Vivianne Crowley is the author of numerous books on the Craft. Her 1989 best-selling book, *The Old Religion in the New Age,* was revised in 1996 and published under the title *The Old Religion in the New Millennium.* She is known for her presentation of Wiccan concepts written in a style easily understood by both beginners and advanced practitioners of the Craft.

91. B. The Pagan Way was not a coven. It was a series of informal introductory classes that were open to the general public. It was formed in response to a rapidly growing interest in Paganism. With no formal initiation or membership requirements, Pagan Way provided an alternative to traditional covens, many of which could not accommodate the large amount of interest. Pagan Ways were formed simultaneously in two cities: Minot, North Dakota, and Philadelphia, Pennsylvania. From there they spread over the United States. The rituals and background materials were never copyrighted but instead were placed in the public domain. Some occult stores and individuals still offer Pagan Way classes to the public.

92. B. Macha NightMare is a member of the Reclaiming Collective. She coauthored *The Pagan Book of Living and Dying* (1999).

    For Your Learning Enjoyment: Judy Harrow is the author of *Wiccan Covens* (Citadel Press, 1999).

93. B. Witches and Pagans were well represented at the Parliament of World Religions in 1993. This event (the only other one that ever occurred took place in 1893) was a gathering of the leaders of world faiths for sharing information and addressing concerns. One or two groups left the Parliament in protest to our being there. At first, the theologians in attendance thought we were loony. But after a few days of hard questioning, they recognized what we were doing and that we are a legitimate religion. Deborah Ann Light, who is a member of Circle, Covenant of the Goddess, and the Fellowship of Isis, signed the Parliament's statement of religious tolerance as a representative of the Pagan and Craft community. Olivia Robertson, of the Fellowship of Isis, was one of those who addressed the Parliament. A permit for a full blue moon circle was originally rejected by the city of Chicago, only to have the ACLU, the Archdiocese of Chicago in the person of Cardinal Bernardin—the first time

in two thousand years that the church stood up for the Witches—and other members of the Parliament step forward to object. The permit was granted, and more than three hundred people, from a wide variety of faiths, joined hands and participated in the landmark event.

 ## TOTAL YOUR POINTS
Chapter 3, section 5: The Modern Magical Movement

_____ Total number of questions 51–93 answered correctly

Multiply the total number of questions 51–93 answered correctly by 2. This will give you your total number of points for chapter 3, section 5:

_____ X 2 = _____
Total number of questions   Total score, chapter 3,
51–93 answered correctly   section 5

Total possible points for chapter 3, section 5 = 86

SECTION 6

Our Wiccan and Pagan Elders —Trivia Pursuit!

94. **D.** The sexy Janet Farrar was on the screen and walked the "catwalk."

95. **C.** Arnold Crowther began working stage magic at a young age. His interest in the occult began when he met Gerald Gardner around 1939 and developed a friendship. He refused Gardner's invitation to be initiated into the Craft, claiming that he was waiting for a special person to do that deed. She finally arrived in the late 1950s in the form of his wife, Patricia Crowther.

   For Your Learning Enjoyment: Jeff McBride is a worldwide-noted stage magician who does blend magical themes with magick. He often plays in Los Vegas and Atlantic City.

His breathtaking performance is well worth the price of a ticket!

96. A. Margot Adler's grandfather was Dr. Alfred Adler, a renowned psychiatrist. Her father and aunt are also psychiatrists.

97. C. Starhawk's real name is Miriam Simos, otherwise known as Mimi to her near and dear friends.

98. A. Z. Budapest fought but lost her case. Nine years later, the law prohibiting psychic readings was repealed.

99. D. Isaac Bonewits. He is the only one to do so, because the campus, out of embarrassment from the publicity, banned the topic from its individual group study program.

100. B. Stewart Farrar was introduced to Wicca in 1969 when, as a reporter for the *Reveille,* he was given the job of interviewing Alex and Maxine Sanders. He liked what he heard and kept coming back, eventually being initiated by Alex and Maxine.

101. C. On July 19, 1988, Margot Adler and Dr. John Gliedman were married in a Wiccan ceremony, with Selena Fox as the Officiant. Their wedding was published on the society page of *The New York Times.* My husband Tom's and my wedding was not included in the *Times,* although my first marriage, to Peter Hoffer, had been scheduled to be carried. We were bumped off the page at the last minute by the wedding of a kindergarten teacher whose entire class participated in the wedding ceremony.

102. C. Gwydion Pendderwen (1946–1982) cofounded the Faerie Tradition with Victor Anderson, but he was also well known as a Celtic bard whose songs and stories still touch the souls of many Wiccans and Pagans long after his untimely death. It is hard to imagine but, Gwydion Pendderwen worked for the IRS.

103. D. Cecil Williamson.

104. A. Valiente read an article about the opening of Williamson's Museum of Witchcraft on the Isle of Man. In it was mentioned a coven in the New Forest area, which is where she happened to live. She mailed a letter to Williamson expressing her interest in Witchcraft and asking for information. Williamson passed the letter on to Gerald Gardner, who then arranged for a meeting.

105. C. Violet Mary Firth.

106. C. Brosseau.

107. B. Dafo.

108. C. With Witchcraft still a crime in England in 1949, Gardner published his novel under the pen name of Scire.

109. B. The Susan B. Anthony Coven.

110. A. An entertainer, doing stand-up comedy.

111. C. Compost and Raving.

112. B. Macha NightMare, the author of *The Pagan Book of Living and Dying*.

113. D. Victor Anderson.

114. B. Isaac Bonewits was introduced to Druidism through his roommate, Robert Larson, an alumnus of Carleton College and Druid through RDNA. They established a grove in Berkeley, California, and Bonewits later became the Archdruid of the order. Bonewits went on in 1983 to found Ár nDraíocht Féin, a Druid organization that includes clergy training. He is the author of *Real Magic* (1971; 1979).

 TOTAL YOUR POINTS
Chapter 3, section 6: Our Wiccan and Pagan Elders—Trivia Pursuit!

_____ Total number of questions 94–114 answered correctly

Multiply the total number of questions 94–114 answered correctly by 2. This will give you your total number of points for chapter 3, section 6:

_____ X 2 = _____
Total number of questions   Total score, chapter 3,
94–114 answered correctly   section 6

Total possible points for chapter 3, section 5 = 42

TOTALING CHAPTER 3

Add together your final scores from each section in chapter 3:

_____ Chapter 3, section 1—Witchcraft in the Ages
+ _____ Chapter 3, section 2—Witchcraft and the Law
+ _____ Chapter 3, section 3—The Burning Times
+ _____ Chapter 3, section 4—The Witch Hysteria in the U.S.
+ _____ Chapter 3, section 5—Modern Magical Movement
+ _____ Chapter 3, section 6—Wiccan and Pagan Elders

= [_____] Grand total for chapter 3

This is the number you will carry forward to the end of the book!

Total possible points for chapter 3 = 228

4

Burn Two Candles and Call Me in the Morning

Spellcraft

Witches are the magic workers. We create change through the altering of consciousness and physical reality in accordance with will. This is also called enchantment, spellcraft, and healing work. How and why it works is a mystery. Many things that were once known as magical practices and theories are now called science—including math, quantum physics, and modern medicine! For our purposes, spellcraft is using knowledge of hidden forces and elements to aid in the magical and physical working. The energies and tools used can look as mundane as the day of the week or a weed in the yard. They can also be as complex as the appropriate colors of candles for the working or the cycle of the moon on which to work the magic. This chapter tests your knowledge of spellworking—from the general principles and theories of how and why it works, to the various means to craft the art of change.

SECTION 1

Working Magic—In Principle and in Theory

1. To enchant something literally means to
   a. bewitch

    b. make something prettier

    c. spellbind with singing

    d. control another's will

2. What is a spell?
   a. a period of time
   b. mixing together different magical ingredients
   c. the speaking of magical words
   d. a wish sent with intent

3. Spells are used to
   a. figure out your income tax
   b. boil an egg
   c. make things happen
   d. change your hair color

4. Of the following, which is *not* a spell?
   a. blowing out the candles on a birthday cake
   b. plucking the petals off a flower while reciting, "he loves me, he loves me not"
   c. lighting a candle for Mother Mary with a prayer requesting aid
   d. after spilling salt, sprinkling a pinch over your shoulder

5. The best time to do magic to bring about change is when you are
   a. really angry, because it will add extra energy to your spell
   b. not sure of what you want, because it will help bring you clarity
   c. sick or tired, because working magic will make you feel better
   d. clear about your intent, rested, and grounded

6. Why shouldn't you do a spell to make someone fall in love with you?
   a. it is unethical to manipulate another person's will
   b. go for it—there is no reason why you can't
   c. the ties are so hard to break
   d. what looks cute today may not be appealing tomorrow

7. The difference between "high" magic and "low" magic is
   a. one is of the Priests in the temple, the other the Witch
   b. one is formal ritual, while the other is more simple or everyday
   c. the voice tone
   d. one is done on hilltops, the other in valleys

8. This is a way of working magic in which a small piece of an object can be used to affect the whole object:
   a. signatures
   b. sympathetic magic
   c. contagious magic
   d. empathic magic

9. Contagious magic is
   a. chaotic energy that hasn't been grounded properly
   b. when a spell accidentally gets transmitted to people other than those intended
   c. the magic essence contained in an object rubbing off onto other things
   d. a spell gone wrong that affects other workings

10. In this form of magic, objects that resemble each other can affect each other; an effect resembles its cause:
    a. homeopathic magic
    b. Newtonian magic
    c. sympathetic magic
    d. impersonation magic

11. If you are practicing thaumaturgy, you're
    a. fusing two or more types of magic together
    b. working fire magic
    c. working magic
    d. creating temperature fluxes

12. In this form of magic, the energy doesn't come from just within yourself. Instead, you get your God or Goddess riled up about what you want, and then he or she provides the juice working through you:

a. possessive
b. prayer
c. theurgy
d. antagonistic/motivational

13. A flask or other container into which the victim of a Witch's curse voids the spell is called a
   a. catchall
   b. spittoon
   c. belching bag
   d. farting bottle

14. This bodily fluid was considered a potent ingredient in folk charms and counterspells:
   a. blood
   b. spit
   c. tears
   d. urine

15. A glamour is
   a. cosmetics
   b. a spell to deceive the eyes
   c. a sexy High Priestess
   d. a book of spells

16. A charm is
   a. a magical tune to bring luck
   b. a breakfast cereal
   c. a spell to infatuate someone
   d. a magical word, phrase, or personal object that contains power

17. An object that has been empowered to protect the wearer by keeping away bad luck is a
   a. talisman
   b. charm
   c. amulet
   d. gun

18. Once empowered, these objects are often carried or worn as a means of attracting something to the carrier:
    a. charm
    b. amulet
    c. glyph
    d. talisman

19. This character or pictograph is carried or worn as protection from bad luck
    a. rune
    b. glyph
    c. talisman
    d. charm

20. The flip side of the spellcasting trade was providing one of these for folks who believed a malicious spell had been placed upon them:
    a. anti-bad-luck amulet
    b. countercharm
    c. talisman
    d. advice

21. Hex signs are often beautiful signs and symbols used to
    a. keep the fox out of the henhouse
    b. keep milk from curdling
    c. return malicious magic back to the sender
    d. protect against lightning and grant fertility

22. These spells are meant to contain and restrict:
    a. curses
    b. binding
    c. love
    d. protection

23. A magical potion, usually made of wine or tea and mixed with herbs, that causes a person to fall in love with another is a
    a. tissane

b. philter

c. aphrodisiac

d. love potion number 9

24. What is a Witch cake?
    a. dark chocolate with chocolate frosting and sprinkles
    b. a cake made with the victim's urine, used to find the caster of a curse
    c. a sacred cake used at May Day to find love
    d. an oatmeal and honey cake, buried with a personal item to draw away a curse

25. A Witch bottle is a charm to
    a. protect against evil sprits and eliminate a curse
    b. protect against lightning
    c. trap a Witch
    d. bring good luck to the home

26. This humanlike doll can be used in sympathetic magic, especially in distant healing work:
    a. bridie doll
    b. voodoo doll
    c. poppet
    d. corn dolly

27. This personal object has often been made into an amulet of strength, sovereignty, and protection:
    a. pin
    b. pendant
    c. ring
    d. watch fob

28. Dating back to second-century Rome, this is one of the oldest-known charms:
    a. horseshoe
    b. four-leaf clover
    c. abracadabra
    d. nails

29. When using poppets for magic, what do you do with the poppet once the magic is done?
    a. burn it
    b. take it apart
    c. give it to a child
    d. bury it

30. An inscribed wax talisman used in magic is called
    a. an almadel
    b. a seal
    c. a candle
    d. a diskus

SECTION 2

Hitting the "C" Notes—Cords, Candles, and Color Magic

31. Cord magic is used for
    a. S&M play
    b. barbershop quartets
    c. binding intentions
    d. macramé

32. Which is traditionally the correct order for tying the knots in cord magic? *(1 = first knot tied, 2=second knot tied, and so on)*

    ⊗ ⊗ ⊗ ⊗ ⊗ ⊗ ⊗ ⊗ ⊗
    a. 1 2 3 4 5 6 7 8 9

    ⊗ ⊗ ⊗ ⊗ ⊗ ⊗ ⊗ ⊗ ⊗
    b. 4 6 2 8 1 9 3 7 5

    ⊗ ⊗ ⊗ ⊗ ⊗ ⊗ ⊗ ⊗ ⊗
    c. 1 6 4 8 3 9 5 7 2

    ⊗ ⊗ ⊗ ⊗ ⊗ ⊗ ⊗ ⊗ ⊗
    d. 8 7 5 3 1 2 4 6 9

33. Colors are important to magical workings because
    a. different colors resonate with different energies
    b. they remind you of what your intent is
    c. they keep you from getting the candles mixed up on your altar
    d. they're cool

34. What does it mean to "dress" a candle?
    a. choose a color
    b. wrap a ribbon around it
    c. inscribe it, anoint it with oils, and charge it with intent
    d. fit a small tuxedo onto the candle

35. When applying oils onto a candle, you should start _____ and move _____ .
    a. in the center; outward
    b. at one end; to the other end
    c. at each end; to the center
    d. by immersion; quickly to a towel to dry

36. For candle magic, it is preferred that the candle be made out of
    a. tallow
    b. beeswax
    c. petroleum
    d. paraffin

37. If you need to extinguish a magical candle before it has burned to the socket, what is the preferred method?
    a. snuffing
    b. pinching
    c. blowing
    d. either a or b

38. It is said that a blue flame is a sign of
    a. divine favor
    b. a wick that needs to be shortened
    c. spirit presence
    d. truth

Color My World

39. Realizing that colors can be completely personal, match each color with its most common associations (1 point per correct answer):

a. white   _____   1. lust, strength, vigor, courage

b. blue   _____   2. stability, grounding in reality, animals

c. green   _____   3. love, friendship, romance

d. yellow   _____   4. purification, protection, healing, spirit

e. orange   _____   5. removal of blockages, banishing, the mystery

f. purple   _____   6. psychic abilities, power

g. red   _____   7. courage, concentration, success

h. brown   _____   8. tranquillity, emotional healing, peace

i. pink   _____   9. joy, happiness, confidence

j. black   _____   10. growth, prosperity, fertility

SECTION 3

Pen to Paper—Magical Scripts

40. Magical writing, alphabets, or symbols have been used by Ceremonial Magicians and Witches for centuries as a manner of
a. guarding the secrets
b. empowering something with intent
c. subconscious programming
d. all of the above

41. As described by Robert Graves in his book *The White Goddess,* this series of symbols makes up a form of an alphabet that he claims to be the oldest form of writing in Celtic Ireland:

a. Ogam
b. runes
c. cuneiform
d. Pictish Swirl

42. Which of the following is *not* one of the sacred trees in Tree Alphabet?
a. elder
b. hazel
c. alder
d. maple

43. This is most commonly referred to as the Witches Alphabet:
a. Germanic Runes
b. Theban
c. cuneiform
d. twengar

44. Translate the following from the Theban:

ᛉᛏᛂ ᛉᛏᘮᘮᛩ ᛗᘮᛏᛏᛉᛂ

45. A sigil is, in magic practice,
a. a magical sign conferring power
b. the written part of a talisman or charm
c. a symbol representing a specific idea
d. a hieroglyph used for magical purposes

46. The most powerful sigil in Wicca is
a. runic cross
b. a pentacle
c. Tree of Life
d. ankh

47. Runes are
a. letter disks used in gambling
b. symbols of power
c. an ancient Scandinavian magical language
d. characters or symbols used in divination and writing

48. Translate the following Germanic Runes:

SECTION 4
Working With Herbs

Knowledge of herbs for both magical and medicinal purposes has
been one of the central pieces of folk magic through the ages. The
medicinal use of herbs most likely started evolving during our
hunter-gatherer stage of development. It would have been noticed
that certain plants, when eaten, also seemed to ease illness. As agriculture developed, so did the cultivation of these helpful plants.
Over time, some people developed the talents for identification of
disease and preparation of herbal remedies. They became the first
"cunning men/women," or "wise men/women." The fact that
these people could cure sickness would have appeared magical,
hence the connection between plant, magic, and healer developed.

There are hundreds of books on the medicinal and magical uses
of herbs. I'm listing just a few of the general herbs, both magical
and medicinal.

SECTION 4A
Working With Herbs—Medicinal Herbs

*Warning: This section is not intended to give medical advice.
Knowledge of herbal remedies does not replace medical science or
common sense. Some magical herbs, in fact, are poisonous if taken
internally or handled improperly. Always research herbal properties
before using and check with your doctor about them.*

49. What time of day is the proper time to harvest flower and
     leaf herbs?
     a. early morning

   b. late morning
   c. afternoon
   d. twilight

50. When should roots be harvested?
    a. spring
    b. midsummer
    c. after the first frost
    d. winter

51. These are the traditional tools for mixing herbs:
    a. chalice and athame
    b. bucket and hammer
    c. mixing bowl and spoon
    d. mortar and pestle

52. Also called hag's taper, this herb can be used as a torch, to ease a chest cold, or to kill fish:
    a. loosestrife
    b. licorice
    c. sunflower
    d. mullein

53. With this herb, you can disinfect your floors and banish demons while breaking up your head congestion!
    a. lavender
    b. hound's-tongue
    c. eucalyptus
    d. valerian

54. Which herb would you *not* put into a tea to calm your nerves?
    a. valerian
    b. skullcap
    c. blackberry
    d. chamomile

55. Which of the following would you *not* use for a stomach ailment?
    a. ginger

  b. catnip
  c. clove
  d. asarum

56. What herb did Julius Caesar use to treat his baldness?
  a. rosemary
  b. hops
  c. ginger
  d. vervain

57. This can counter the poisonous effects of hemlock:
  a. cohosh
  b. coffee
  c. self-heal
  d. yarrow

58. It has been known for about two thousand years that the bark of this tree reduces pain and fevers. The synthetic form of its chemical compound is commonly known as aspirin:
  a. oak
  b. willow
  c. rowan
  d. hawthorn

59. This plant is very edible and nutritious. It can be used to make coffee, tea, wine, and two kinds of dye, and it also helps with kidney troubles—yet most homeowners spend a lot of time trying to get rid of it!
  a. coltsfoot
  b. dandelion
  c. shepherd's purse
  d. ground ivy

60. This popular plant is enjoyed in everything from pickling to garnish. It is also a very powerful antibiotic. Mixed with sage in a tea form, it helps soothe a common cold. During summer, it can keep mosquitoes at bay:
  a. lavender
  b. St.-John's-wort

    c. goldenrod
    d. garlic

61. Which herb would you *not* take if you are pregnant?
    a. tansy
    b. celery
    c. ergot
    d. all of the above

62. Of these four herbs, which one has *not* been used as an aphrodisiac?
    a. damiana
    b. pussywillow
    c. fenugreek
    d. garlic

Herbal Preparations

63. Match up each preparation method with its proper name (1 point per method):

    a. tincture   _____   1. tea-soaked bandage
    b. tisane   _____   2. placed directly onto the skin
    c. decoction   _____   3. boiled tea
    d. compress   _____   4. oils or fats
    e. poultice   _____   5. soaked in alcohol
    f. ointment   _____   6. tea

Healing Properties

64. Match each term with its properties (1 point per term):

    a. alterative   _____   1. tightens body tissue
    b. antispasmodic _____   2. blood cleanser
    c. aphrodisiac   _____   3. promotes mucus discharge
    d. aromatic   _____   4. calming to nerves
    e. astringent   _____   5. soothes mucous membranes

f. demulcent   _____ 6. relieves cramps
g. expectorant _____ 7. excites
h. febrifuge   _____ 8. reduces fever
i. nervine   _____ 9. affects scent
j. stimulant   _____ 10. increases sexual desire

SECTION 4B

Working With Herbs—Herbal Magic

65. What is the proper tool to collect herbs for magical work-ings?
    a. kitchen shears
    b. athame
    c. sickle
    d. bolline or silver knife

66. This is a small cloth bag stuffed with herbs that induce sleep or psychic visions while asleep:
    a. astral cushion
    b. psychic pillow
    c. dream pillow
    d. dream cushion

67. What would you *not* put in a travel protection sachet to be hung in a car?
    a. nutmeg
    b. lemon verbena
    c. juniper
    d. comfrey

68. What is a traditional reason to burn rue?
    a. restful sleep
    b. protection against dog bites
    c. protection against the evil eye
    d. purification of the ritual space

69. Of the following, which is *not* safe to burn in an enclosed space?
    a. camphor

b. betony
c. dragon's blood
d. mace

70. Which of the following would *not* go into a love attraction spell?
    a. roses
    b. pansy
    c. heather
    d. cinnamon

71. You need a job, or you're unsure about the one that you have. Which of the following has *not* traditionally been used in working employment spells?
    a. pecan
    b. hemp
    c. lucky hand
    d. devil's shoestring

72. This traditional herb is found in wedding bouquets, including those for the queens of England:
    a. yarrow
    b. violets
    c. meadowsweet
    d. lavender

73. When people went to "gather in the May," what were they collecting?
    a. rowan blossoms
    b. hawthorn blossoms
    c. lilacs
    d. apple blossoms

74. According to folklore, what tool do you need in order to harvest mandrake root?
    a. a dog
    b. a golden sickle
    c. a kris knife
    d. a scarf

SECTION 5

Timing Is Everything—The Nights

75. In some traditions, liminal times, those of twilight and sunrise, are the optimal moments to work magic because
    a. it's quiet and you can work without interruption
    b. it won't interrupt the rest of your day or night
    c. it's the time for fey folk
    d. it's the moment of transformation between light and dark

76. To do magic that involves banishing or removing of obstacles, you would best be served to do it during a
    a. waxing moon
    b. full moon
    c. waning moon
    d. new moon

77. To do magic that increases your luck, fertility, or health, involves anything that you wish to draw to you, you would be best to do your working during a
    a. waxing moon
    b. full moon
    c. waning moon
    d. new moon

78. The full moon is the height of psychic powers. It would be a good time to work which kind of magic?
    a. divination
    b. love magic
    c. dream work
    d. whatever you have need of

79. When the moon is hidden, it's a good time to work which kind of magic?
    a. mystery, initiation
    b. banishing bad habits
    c. growth, abundance
    d. new adventure, communication

80. What does it mean when the moon is "void of course"?
    a. bad directions
    b. when a planet appears to be rotating in the backward direction or motion
    c. the blank periods during the moon's transition between astrological signs
    d. when the moon rises before the sun sets

Timing Is Everything—The Days

81. Saturday is named after the Roman God Saturn. It would therefore be an auspicious day to work which kind of magic?
    a. finding a new love
    b. removing of obstacles
    c. increasing fertility
    d. quick action

82. Tuesday is named after the Norse God Tyr, whom classical writers associate with which Roman God?
    a. Mercury
    b. Jupiter
    c. Mars
    d. Apollo

83. Which day of the week would be the most auspicious for magical workings involving vitality, male energy, power, increased prosperity?
    a. Monday
    b. Wednesday
    c. Thursday
    d. Sunday

84. Thursday is Thor's day. Classical writers linked him with Jupiter. It would therefore be an auspicious day to work which kind of magic?
    a. self-improvement

    b. luck with a lawsuit
    c. divination
    d. happy home

85. Named after Wodon, Wednesday is associated with the Roman God Mercury. It would therefore be an auspicious day to work which kind of magic?
    a. sex
    b. gardening
    c. communication
    d. health

86. She is the Venus of Norse mythology and Friday is Her day. Who is She?
    a. Freyr
    b. Frita
    c. Fjorgnn
    d. Freya

87. Which day would be the most auspicious for workings involving women's issues and health, mothers, fertility, and nurturing?
    a. Sunday
    b. Monday
    c. Wednesday
    d. Friday

SECTION 6

Crafting the Art of Magical Change

Note: Magic is very subjective and personal. Rituals and working magic can actually be done on any day and time. If you need something immediately, you're not going to wait until the moon is in the exact point in its cycle on just the right day of the week. The answers to the following case studies are generalizations, the "if you were in a perfect world" scenarios. Feel free to disagree with my answers—but if you do, make sure you have a firm, good reason in your mind why you would do it differently! Sometimes it will be a matter of picking which answer is the least wrong.

88. Your next-door neighbor is driving you nuts with the high volume of his TV late at night. What can you do to help alleviate the problem?
    a. banishing spell, so he'll clear out and give you some sleep
    b. love magic, so he'll find a new girlfriend and be focused on her instead of David Letterman
    c. prosperity spell, so he'll get enough money to move away to another neighborhood
    d. communication: a knock on the door with a request for quiet

89. You are in desperate need of a job. Of the following, which is the best course of magical action?
    a. do candle magic to send out a psychic call for a job
    b. do chanting and power raising directed toward finding a job
    c. empower the paper of your resumé, that it will get into the hands of the people who need to review it, and mail it out
    d. burn a copy of your resumé, sending it out onto the winds

90. Your friend is burning with jealously over an old flame. What would be the most auspicious time for her to do a ritual to banish these intense emotions and regain balance in her life?
    a. a new moon, at midnight, preferably on a Saturday
    b. a waning moon, at twilight, preferably on a Friday
    c. a waxing moon, night, preferably on a Sunday
    d. a full moon, night, preferably on a Wednesday

91. Time to lose weight! What would be an auspicious time to start your diet?
    a. a full moon, midnight, preferably on a Tuesday
    b. a new moon, midday, preferably on a Wednesday

c. a waxing moon, twilight, preferably on a Saturday
d. a waning moon, dawn, preferably on a Thursday

92. You need more money, a raise, or career advancement. What would be the most auspicious time for you to do a ritual to help you in this goal?
a. a waning moon, at dawn, preferably on a Monday
b. a new moon, at midnight, preferably on a Wednesday
c. a waxing moon, at midday, preferably on Sunday
d. a full moon, at twilight, preferably on a Friday

93. What would be the most auspicious time to do a purification ritual to open your heart and connect with the God/dess?
a. a full moon, twilight, preferably on a Monday
b. a new moon, midnight, preferably on a Tuesday
c. a waxing moon, dawn, preferably on a Sunday
d. a waning moon, night, preferably on a Saturday

94. You've been lonely too long. Your life is in order, your emotional being is balanced; it's time for a partner to share the years. What would be the most auspicious time for you to send out a heart call for a new relationship?
a. a full moon, midnight, preferably on a Saturday
b. a waxing moon, dawn, preferably on a Friday
c. a new moon, twilight, preferably on a Monday
d. a waning moon, midday, preferably on a Sunday

SECTION 7

Working Magic—Actual Folk Charms, Myths, and Practices

All are worth 1 point each!

95. This folk tradition was used whenever cream refused to turn to butter as a means to stop whoever was hexing it:
a. inserting a heated iron poker
b. toss a charm into the butter

    c. inscribe a rune onto the bucket

    d. yell a mind curse at the cream

96. This charm, called an alrum, was made for good luck and for protection from angry fey folk. It is created by forming a solar cross with twigs from which tree?

    a. hawthorn

    b. apple

    c. rowan

    d. oak

97. To keep your house safe from lightning, each year you should

    a. save a piece of the Yule log

    b. tie silver streamers from the roofing

    c. libate the house, and all within it, with good whiskey

    d. bury Ostara eggs at the four points of the property

98. This was done to prevent sparks from leaping out of the fireplace:

    a. crossing the poker and tongs before the hearth

    b. closing the flue

    c. burning thirteen pieces of oak

    d. drawing a sigil in the ash

99. To escape the seven-year curse created by the breaking of a mirror,

    a. smash it into tiny pieces and bury it in the graveyard

    b. directly after breaking it, turn counterclockwise three times

    c. glue the pieces back together

    d. wrap the pieces in white cloth and carefully tend them for the seven years

100. To sleep well each evening, your bed should be set so your body lies

    a. east to west

    b. west to east

    c. north to south

    d. south to north

101. This is hung in the kitchen, not as something to eat but for protection, because it will absorb any negative energy:
    a. mandrake root
    b. rope of garlic or onions
    c. ginseng root
    d. lemongrass braid

102. It is considered very unlucky to ever run out of this, because if you do loss of wealth and health will surely follow:
    a. pepper
    b. cinnamon
    c. salt
    d. sugar

Answers to Chapter 4

Unless otherwise stated, give yourself *2 points for each correct answer.* At the end of the chapter, add together your total points from each section to get your final score for the chapter. This number will be carried forward to the end of the book for a final tally!

SECTION 1

Working Magic—In Principle and in Theory

1. C. The word *enchantment* comes from the Latin *incantare*, meaning "to sing," and thus literally means to spellbind with singing.

2. D. A spell is a spoken or written formula that is magically intended to cause or influence a particular course of events.

The root for *spell* comes from the German word *spiel*, which means "play" or "story."

3. C. Whether it's done through chanting, dancing, breathwork, writing, empowering of an object, or shouting from the rooftops, the purpose of a spell is to facilitate change.

4. B. The plucking of petals off a flower while reciting, "he loves me, he loves me not" is a form of divination. While some people may object to the candle for Mother Mary, in my opinion it is still an act done for the purpose of facilitating change (healing), through the power or grace of the Goddess.

5. D. Magic is real. The energy comes from you. If you're not clear about your intent, your magic will not be focused. If you're angry when you do your working, you may do something that you'll regret later when you've had time to calm down. If you're sick or tired, you won't have the energy to put into your magic. The best time to work magic is when you're psychically and emotionally in balance and your intent is clear.

6. A. Many Witches consider it highly unethical to work manipulative magic upon another's will. It can also have some drastic and unexpected results. I know of one young lady who cast some strong love magic spells on a young man. It worked, and they were together for a few years, during which time he developed a severe drug problem. Despite her attempts, she couldn't get rid of him! Even after he died from a drug overdose, she remained bound to him with his spirit haunting her. Most frightening were his frequent requests that she join his shade on the other side! It took a lot of work to sever the tie. If you want to attract someone, do some work on yourself. If you are truly ready for a relationship, you can send out a heart call to the God/dess without a direct focus on an individual. If the one you are lusting after is meant to be with you, he or she will hear it and re-

spond of his or her own accord. Or you may get a pleasant surprise and find out that the person you need is actually someone you hadn't previously considered.

7. B. High magic is a more formal and ritualized style, often taking lots of time. In contrast, low magic is more the everyday sort of work, like making soup for a sick friend and adding a bit of healing magic to the pot.

8. B. Sympathetic magic is popular way of working magical energy. It is the idea that a part of an object can affect its greater whole—for example, that using bits of an ill person's hair when working healing magic will help transmit the magic to that person. This method is also employed in poppet spells. Bits of physical pieces of the intended recipient of the magic, such as hair or clothing, are often added to the poppet along with other herbs or magical ingredients, creating a psychic tie between the doll and the person.

9. C. An object that was once in contact with another object can retain some of the original object's essence even after being removed from that object and thus can either affect the original object or bring some of its specialness back to the user. For example, a medal that has touched a sacred statue may be removed from the statue, but it can still carry within it part of the essences of the spirit inherent in the statue.

10. A. Homeopathic or imitative magic, according to Frazier in *The Golden Bough,* is based on the idea or law of similarities—"like produces like."[1] For example, to find a new home, you could draw a picture of house and work magic focused on that image. Or, in Frazier's example, destroying a picture of an enemy will destroy that enemy.

11. C. The word *thaumaturgy* comes from the Greek *thau-*

[1]Frazer, Sir James George. *The Golden Bough: A Study in Magic and Religion.* New York: MacMillan Company, 1960, p. 14.

mato, meaning "miracle" or "wonder." So to practice thau-maturgy is to work magic.

12. C. Theurgy is working with the God/dess energy, drawing into yourself the Divine energy so that your will and the Divine work together to bring about change.

13. D. A farting bottle is a bottle or other container into which a victim of a Witch's curse would "pass wind." The curse would be expelled with the fart. The bottle was then sealed and buried in the ground, thereby breaking or containing the curse.

14. D. Urine was used in many folk charms and counterspells. Early physicians used it as a diagnostic tool, even judging the prognosis for recovery on the color and condition of the patient's urine. Cunning men and women added urine to magical remedies to cure as well as to detect a curse. Boiling the urine was also a popular means to eradicate a curse.

15. B. The movie *The Craft* made this term familiar to American youth. It is a spell to deceive the eyes. It's for when a bit of makeup just isn't going to do the trick.

16. D. There are charms in existence for just about every desire or need. It is a word, phrase, or object that has magical power to help heal or hurt. It can be verbal (as in a prayer), worn, written, carried; it can be self-made, created, or self-identified (as in a lucky pair of socks). Even medieval churches promoted the use of holy charms such as rosaries and holy relics.

17. C. An amulet is an object that has been inscribed or charged to protect the wearer by keeping away harm or bad luck. Egyptians, Assyrians, Babylonians, Arabs, and Hebrews all placed importance in amulets. Egyptian amulets that many are familiar with are ankhs, which represent everlasting life, and the eye of Horus, used for protection. In Wicca, the pentacle is the most powerful of amulets.

18. D. While amulets protect the wearer by keeping negativity away, talismans attract energies. They are objects that possess magical or supernatural power, frequently inherent within the object, that is transmitted to the owner. For example, precious stones have always been considered talismans, each having its own magical or curative powers endowed by Nature. Talismans usually only perform a single function or type of magic.

19. B. A glyph is a written or drawn symbol, such as a rune, that is carried to protect the wearer against bad luck.

20. B. A countercharm is a device by which a person could counteract the ill or malevolent effects of Witchcraft and guard against any future attacks. Amulets made from herbs or human-made objects such as horseshoes would be hung above the threshold of a house as a form of countercharm.

21. D. Hex signs are round magical signs and symbols used by the Pennsylvania Dutch, primarily to protect against the ill effects of Witchcraft and lightning, and to ensure fertility.

22. B. There was a time when it was believed that a Witch who couldn't curse wasn't a real Witch. While some still hold this to be true, the majority of modern Witches believe that cursing or binding another's will is unethical and a breaking of the Wiccan Rede. Still, not all binding spells are for evil or harmful purposes! A binding can be done to seal the magic into an amulet or talisman, to prevent a miscarriage, or as protection to keep a bad situation contained without binding the will of another.

23. B. A philter is a magical potion that causes a person to fall in love with another. It traditionally consists of wine, tea, or water infused with herbs or drugs. Another common ingredient is root of mandrake (a poisonous member of the nightshade family). This is considered unethical magic by many Witches.

24. B. Making a cake with the urine of the afflicted was a pop-

ular way of detecting the caster of a curse. In Salem in 1692, when the girls were first affected, Mary Sibly (the aunt of one of the afflicted girls) asked Tituba to bake such a cake. The cake is traditionally thrown into the fire as a means of breaking the enchantment or fed to a dog, which will either exhibit signs of the curse or lead people to the Witch who placed it.

25. A. This is a common charm used in folk magic to protect against evil spirits and magical attack, and to counteract spells cast by Witches. A little bottle is filled with bits of the victim's urine, hair or nail clippings, pins, needles, and nails. The bottle is buried beneath a house's hearth or threshold to either break the spell or protect against malicious magic. If a bottle is made to counter a spell, the Witch who supposedly cast it will be bound and suffer great discomfort. Sometimes the bottle was thrown into the fire; when it exploded, the Witch was supposedly killed.

26. C. A poppet is a magical doll made for spellcasting. It is often made out of cloth, wax, wood, or clay. The doll substitutes, in a form of sympathetic magic, for the person who is the object of the spell. It is a type of image magic in which the doll is magically connected to the individual for whom the work is being crafted. Poppets can be used for many purposes, including healing, self-focus or change, and distance work.

    For Your Learning Enjoyment: Bridie, also called the biddy doll, is made at Imbolc in honor of St. Bridget to welcome spring. A corn dolly is a variation on a poppet used to help ensure the fertility of the land. A voodoo doll is the name given to poppets used within the Afro-Caribbean religion.

27. C. Rings are popular items to be made into amulets of power, strength, sovereignty, and protection. In legend, they are also talismans of magic, enabling their wearers to perform supernatural feats such as becoming invisible.

28. C. *Abracadabra* is a magical spell consisting of a single

word. It is inscribed on an amulet or written out on paper in a magical inverted triangle, in which one letter of the word is dropped in each succeeding line, until nothing is left. It's one of the oldest-known charms, dating back to second-century Rome, and is supposed to cure a fever.

29. B. A poppet is created as a representation of a person. It should be treated kindly while the magic is working, and when the magic is complete, the poppet should be gently taken apart, the pieces buried. Because this is sympathetic magic, you should not burn, bury, or drown your poppet!

30. A. The beauty of an almadel is that it can be melted down to destroy the information or release the spell.

TOTAL YOUR POINTS
Chapter 4, section 1: Working Magic

_____ Total number of questions 1–30 answered correctly

Multiply the total number of questions 1–30 answered correctly by 2. This will give you your total number of points for chapter 4, section 1:

_____ X 2 = _____
Total number of questions   Total score, chapter 4,
1–30 answered correctly   section 1

Total possible points for chapter 4, section 1 = 60

SECTION 2

Hitting the "C" Notes—Cords, Candles, and Color Magic

31. C. Often used for binding magic, cord magic is a form of sympathetic magic applied by means of knotted rope. It can be used to inflict harm, such as holding a baby within a

womb (which may be a good thing if there is a risk of miscarriage) or rendering a man impotent. The tying and untying of knots is used to constrain and release energy in many folk magic spells and formulas.

32. C.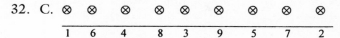

When you are finished tying your knots, the cord is placed in a safe place until you are ready to release the binding. It should be untied starting with the last knot (knot number nine), then the next to last (knot number eight), and so on until all the knots have been released.

33. A. Each color has its own vibration, its own energies, attributes, symbolism, and influence. We perceive colors as being different because of the different light waves that bounce off them. It has been scientifically proven that different colors affect our moods and therefore our intentions. In spells, candles are often burned to release energy or remove obstacles, or as a focus for scrying.

34. C. To dress a candle is to prepare it for magical work. Oil, often essential oils, are applied to the candle. Sigils, runes, or other magical symbols may be carved into it also, further embodying in the candle the intent of the working. In addition to dressing, some spells require the wrapping of a ribbon or string around the candle. This is part of the working, and not necessarily a part of the preparation of the candle.

35. A. Traditionally, the oil is applied starting in the center of the candle and working outward toward the ends.

36. B. Most modern-day candles are made of paraffin. While it's perfectly fine to use these candles, ideally the candles should be made out of beeswax, which is an unadulterated substance.

37. D. It is said that blowing out the flame on a candle lit for

magical purposes will also blow out the magic. This is also viewed by some as being rude to the fire element. Pinching or snuffing is the preferred method of extinguishing the flame. Some people create a vacuum, moving the candle in a quick downward motion, letting the lack of air extinguish the flame.

38. C. According to tradition, a blue flame indicates spirit presence.

Color My World

39. Match each color with its most common association (1 point per correct answer):

    a. white   __4__   purification, protection, healing, spirit
    b. blue   __8__   tranquillity, emotional healing, peace
    c. green   __10__   growth, prosperity, fertility
    d. yellow   __9__   joy, happiness, confidence
    e. orange   __7__   courage, concentration, success
    f. purple   __6__   psychic abilities, power
    g. red   __1__   lust, strength, vigor, courage
    h. brown   __2__   stability, grounding in reality, animals
    i. pink   __3__   love, friendship, romance
    j. black   __5__   removal of blockages, banishing, the mystery

For Further Reading: Charms, Spells & Formulas by Ray T. Malbrough. St. Paul: Llewellyn Publications, 1987.

    TOTAL YOUR POINTS
    Chapter 4, section 2: Hitting the "C" Notes

_____ Total number of questions 31–38 answered correctly

Multiply the total number of questions 31–38 answered correctly by 2:

_____ X 2 = _____

Total number of questions	Total 2-point questions,
31–38 answered correctly	chapter 4, section 2

_____ Total number of 1-point matches, question 39

Add together your 2-point total with your 1-point total:

_____ + _____ = _____

1-point total,	2-point total,	Total score, chapter
question 39	questions 31–38	4, section 2

Total possible points for chapter 4, section 2 = 26

SECTION 3
Pen to Paper—Magical Scripts

40. D. To help keep the secrets from being revealed to noninitiates, magical writing, alphabets, and symbols are used by some Ceremonial Magicians and modern witches for scripting their Books of Shadows. It can also be inscribed onto objects such as tools, candles, talismans, and amulets as a means of empowering the object with intent.

41. A. Ogam, or Ogham, or Ogam Bethlusisnion is a form of writing that was used more for carving than script. Using a centerline, straight lines are drawn above, below, and across to indicate different letters. It has also been called the "Tree Alphabet," because each letter is associated with a tree.

42. D. The maple is indigenous to North America and would therefore not be included on a list of the Celtic trees.

43. B. Theban Script is also known as the Witches Alphabet. Not all Traditions use magical scripts, but of those that do, Theban is the most common.

For Your Learning Enjoyment: Although you can write in Germanic Runes, Witches tend to use them more for crafting talismans or sigils. Cuneiform is a type of wedge-shaped writing used by the Babylonians, Persians, and others.

44. Translation of  : "the magic circle."

45. C.   Sigils are symbols linked to sets of ideas by which spirits or deities may be called into awareness. They can also represent complex concepts or contain entire essences of a spell. The pentacle is the most powerful sigil for contemporary Witchcraft. Other examples are the identifying logos of organizations. It is a visual stimulus that works on the subconscious.

46. B.   A pentacle.

47. D.   The word *rune* means "mystery." There are several types of runes—Germanic, Anglo-Saxon, Scandinavian/Norse, to name just a few. Each rune has a letter and meaning associated with it. They comprise a system used for writing and for divination.

48. Translation: "the song."

TOTAL YOUR POINTS
Chapter 4, section 3: Magical Scripts

_____ Total number of questions 40–48 answered correctly

Multiply the total number of questions 40–48 answered correctly by 2. This will give you your total number of points for chapter 4, section 3:

_____ X 2 = _____
Total number of questions   Total score, chapter 4,
40–48 answered correctly   section 3

Total possible points for chapter 4, section 3 = 18

SECTION 4A

Working With Herbs—Medicinal Herbs

49. B. The flowers and leaves of herbs should be harvested when the dew has dried on the leaves and flowers, not in the early morning or after a rain—moisture will cause them to rot.

50. C. Roots are harvested after the first frost when the energy of the leaves has returned to the root.

51. D. The mortar is the bowl and the pestle is used to grind and combine the herbs.

52. D. The tall and heavy stalk of the mullein plant can be dried, dipped in tallow, and used as a torch. Chopped-up pieces of mullein thrown into a pond can kill the fish. It has also been used to treat bronchitis.

     For Your Learning Enjoyment: The primary use of loose-strife is to alleviate diarrhea. Licorice helps make other concoctions taste a bit better. It is also good for bronchitis or other respiratory troubles. Sunflowers are high in proteins and other minerals.

53. C. The oil found in the leaves of the eucalyptus is highly volatile. It is one of the strongest antiseptics, killing germs and bacteria. The leaves are often put into hot water, and the steam is then inhaled to help break up congestion. It has been used magically to banish demons.

     For Your Learning Enjoyment: Lavender is aromatic, lifts the spirits, and is good for tummy troubles. Hound's tongue root is primarily for diarrhea and insect bites, but it does cause dermatitis in some people. Valerian is the plant from which the sedative Valium was derived. It is a serious nervine, and should be handled with care.

54. C. Blackberry is great if you have diarrhea, but it is not specifically used to calm nerves.

55. D. Asarum is a strong emetic—which means it will have the opposite effect, that of making you vomit.

56. A. Rosemary stimulates the blood flow, which is why Caesar tried it, but it will not aid in male pattern baldness.
    For Your Learning Enjoyment: Hops is an ingredient in beer, and acts as a sedative. Ginger is an all-around good herb, acting to strengthen the system. It is also good for an upset tummy. Vervain has been used to treat asthma, calm the nerves, and reduce fevers.

57. B. Coffee is a stimulant that can counter the poison in hemlock by speeding up and pushing it out of your system.
    For Your Learning Enjoyment: Cohosh should never be taken by a pregnant woman unless a miscarriage is the desired result! It has been used to help force the baby from the womb when the mother is no longer able to deliver. If you have any kind of skin condition, you may want to check out the herb self-heal, because that is its major use. Yarrow was once called the poor man's Band-Aid, as the crushed leaves stop the flow of blood.

58. B. The willow is one of those amazing trees that is multifunctional. Its bark reduces inflammation, fevers, internal bleeding, heartburn, and tummy troubles . . . and that's just on the inside! Outside the body, it can be gargled for throat or gum irritation, used to wash sores and burns, and even take care of your sweating feet!

59. B. All parts of the dandelion are edible. It has been used to make coffee, tea, wine, and dye. Medicinally, it is used as a diuretic, cleansing the kidneys. The French call it *piss-en-lit,* which means "wet the bed."

60. D. Garlic! Goldenseal is another great antibiotic, but it won't do a thing for mosquitoes—and it tastes nasty mixed with sage.

    For Your Learning Enjoyment: St.-John's-wort has been found useful as a mood enhancer. Lavender will relax you and may keep the bugs away, but it isn't an antibiotic.

61. D. This shows how many herbs can have drastic effects on a growing fetus. All those listed can induce an early labor! Be very careful when choosing the herbs you put into your body if you are pregnant.

62. B. Pussywillow is a sexual sedative and antiaphrodisiac.

Herbal Preparations

63. Match up each preparation method with its proper name (1 point per correct match):

a.	tincture	5	soaked in alcohol
b.	tisane	6	tea
c.	decoction	3	boiled tea
d.	compress	1	tea-soaked bandage
e.	poultice	2	placed directly onto the skin
f.	ointment	4	oils or fats

    _____ Total correct matches, question 63

Healing Properties

64. Match each term with its properties (1 point per correct match):

a.	alterative	2	blood cleanser
b.	antispasmodic	6	relieves cramps
c.	aphrodisiac	10	increases sexual desire
d.	aromatic	9	affects scent

e. astringent   __1__   tightens body tissue
f. demulcent   __5__   soothes mucous membranes
g. expectorant   __3__   promotes mucus discharge
h. febrifuge   __8__   reduces fever
i. nervine   __4__   calming to nerves
j. stimulant   __7__   excites

____ Total correct matches, question 64

TOTAL YOUR POINTS
Chapter 4, section 4A: Medicinal Herbs

_____ Total number of questions 49–62 answered correctly

Multiply the total number of questions 49–62 answered correctly by 2:

_____ X 2 = _____
Total number of questions   Total 2-point questions,
49–62 answered correctly   chapter 4, section 4A

____ Total number of 1-point matches, question 63
+ ____ Total number of 1-point matches, question 64
= ____ Total score, 1-point matches

Add together your 2-point total with your 1-point total:

_____ + _____ = _____
1-point total,   2-point total,   Total score, chapter 4,
questions 63 and 64   questions 49–62   section 4A

Total possible points for chapter 4, section 4A = 44

SECTION 4B
Working With Herbs—Herbal Magic

65. D. Bolline, the white-handled knife of the Witch, or a silver knife. Some Witches also set aside a special knife that they dedicate to just harvesting herbs.

66. C. A dream pillow is a small bag, about the size of a small pillowcase, that is stuffed with herbs and placed on top of your pillow to sleep on. Mullein is one of the herbs most commonly placed in a dream pillow, because it keeps away nightmares.

67. A. Comfrey worn or carried protects during a journey. Lemon verbena will keep you from daydreaming while you drive. A sprig of juniper protects against accidents. Nutmeg is used to induce sleep!

68. C. Burned rue wards against the evil eye, malicious spirits, or Witchcraft.

69. A. Although it is an ingredient in many incenses, *pure* camphor is poisonous! What you get in stores is usually processed. Even so, make sure you use it in a limited amount and with the windows open.

70. C. Heather is used to guard against rape by avoiding all acts of passion. Unless you're looking for a strictly platonic relationship, it may not be the best ingredient to put in a sachet to attract love!

71. B. Pecan, devil's shoestring, and lucky hand have all been used for luck in finding and keeping employment. Hemp is used for visions and in love sachets.

72. C. Another name for meadowsweet is bridewort. It is placed in the bouquet of the bride and scattered on the altar for a happy marriage.

73.   B.   The May Pole is traditionally decorated with hawthorn blossoms, which are said to be blooming on Beltane.

74.   A.   The mandrake, which resembles a human body, is considered a very powerful magical root. It is used in love magic or carved into poppets, provides protection, and cures impotency. According to folklore, when a mandrake root is pulled from the ground, it lets out an earsplitting scream that can kill the harvester. In order to avoid this, a string is tied to the root and then tied to a dog. The harvester runs as fast as possible away from the area, leaving the dog to pull up on the root as it tries to follow the harvester, removing the root from the ground. This will then, unfortunately, kill the dog, but it will leave the harvester unharmed.

TOTAL YOUR POINTS
Chapter 4, section 4B: Herbal Magic

_____ Total number of questions 65–74 answered correctly

Multiply the total number of questions 65–74 answered correctly by 2. This will give you your total number of points for chapter 4, section 4B:

_____ X 2 = _____

Total number of questions   Total score, chapter 4,
65–74 answered correctly   section 4B

Total possible points for chapter 4, section 4B = 20

SECTION 5

Timing Is Everything—The Nights

75.   D.   Different times of day hold different kinds of energies. The afternoon, with the sun shining above, offers the full

force of solar power with all its strength and vigor. At midnight, we feel the full energy of the moon and the changes of the cycles. Sunrise and sunset are the moments of transformation between light and dark and are therefore considered by some to be highly magical periods. Sunrise holds new beginnings and hope. Twilight is the letting go into the mystery as the light dims the colors and hides the fine details from view.

76. C. The waning moon, when the full energy of the moon is dispersing, is a good time to banish negativity, illness, bad habits, or anything else that you need to release.

77. A. During the waxing moon, as the moon moves toward its fullness, you can catch some of its growth energy and work any kind of magic that draws things to you and brings them to fruition.

78. D. In Leland's *Aradia,* the Goddess states, "Whenever you have need of anything, once in the month, and when the moon is full, then you shall assemble in some secret place, or in a forest all together join. . . ." It is a general-purpose ritual time, as well as a time to honor the Mother in Her fullness.

79. A. In the darkness of the moon, we can see the inner reflections. It is a time for initiations or revealing of the mysteries, new beginnings, and magic that works toward justice.

80. C. *Void of course* is an astrological term referring to the times when the moon moves out of one astrological sign and enters into a new one. As it travels, there can be a kind of pause, or blank period, when the moon is in no sign or "void" of sign. This can last a few minutes or a day. It isn't a great time to do magic, because the energy can be scattered or unclear.

Timing Is Everything—The Days

81. B. Saturn rules limitations, discipline, discovery, justice, transformation, and structure. It is therefore a good day for workings to eliminate obstacles and limitations, and create balance in your life.

82. C. Mars, also known as Mardi in French, is associated with the Norse God Tyr. Because he is a God of war and victory, magic that centers on courage, action, desire, quick movement, passion, and aggression would work well on Tuesday.

83. D. Sunday is literally the "sun's day." Sunday is the best day for bringing light to an issue. Because it's a strong, masculine day, it suits well for workings that center on men, fathers, and other types of authority figures. Sunday is also a good day for rituals concerning vitality, strength, happiness, or increasing prosperity and power.

84. A. Jupiter rules business, social matters, education, power, wealth, success, abundance, and growth. Thursday would be a good day to work any kind of self-improvement.

85. C. Mercury is the fast-footed messenger to the gods. He is known for his healing wisdom, intelligence, memory, logic, and reasoning. He opens the way for clear communication and self-expression.

86. D. Freya and Venus both hold the romance in magic. Friday, Her day, is a good day to work magic for love, harmony, relationships, loyalty, social activities, balance, and partnerships.
    For Your Learning Enjoyment: Freyr is Freya's twin brother. He is associated with fertility and prosperity. Fjorgyn is an early Nordice fertility Goddess who is thought to be the mother of Thor.

87. B. Monday is the moon's day. This is a great day for work-

ings dealing with women, especially women's health issues and fertility. It is also a good day for connection with the moon's energy, divination, emotions, imagination, and dream work.

TOTAL YOUR POINTS
Chapter 4, section 5: Timing Is Everything

_____ Total number of questions 75–87 answered correctly

Multiply the total number of questions 75–87 answered correctly by 2. This will give you your total number of points for chapter 4, section 5:

_____ X 2 = _____

Total number of questions   Total score, chapter 4,
75–87 answered correctly   section 5

Total possible points for chapter 4, section 5 = 26

SECTION 6
Crafting the Art of Magical Change

Note: Magic is very subjective and personal. The answers to the following case studies are generalizations. Feel free to disagree, but have a firm, good reason in your mind why you would do it differently!

88. D. Doing any magic for people without their request is considered unwise, because it could easily backfire on you. In addition, many Witches consider doing so baneful and unethical. You could do a banishing and then see new neighbors move in who have fourteen children, the oldest of whom loves David Letterman and the youngest of whom gets up at 6:00 A.M. Try a love spell and his new girlfriend might also enjoy late-night TV, then keep you awake until

2:00 A.M. with their constant bumping noises. With prosperity, he might get enough to move but instead decide to
buy a wide-screen TV with a surround sound system! Your
first, and usually simplest, solution is the mundane. Knock
on his door and request that he turn the volume down. If
that doesn't work, then the landlord or police can add a bit
of backing to your appeal. Only after all avenues have been
explored should magic be used.

89. C. Magic isn't easy. It will not solve all of your problems
overnight. Magic requires work, on both the spiritual and
the physical plane. You can do all the magical work you
want, but if your resumé doesn't get out, how is anyone
going to see it? Work must be done on the mundane level,
too! When working toward a goal, be clear about what it is
you want, and don't forget the action that needs to take
place on this plane of reality to help it manifest. You can do
all the other spellwork listed, but if there is no physical
follow-up, the chances of success are limited.

90. A. The new moon is the time for exploring our deepest
fears and angers, and the hour of midnight is prime for ban-
ishments that get to the dark heart of the matter. Saturday is
the day of Saturn, who holds sway over obstacles, limitations, transformation, and self-discovery.

91. D. The waning moon is for releasing and getting rid of bad
habits. Dawn is for beginnings, because the sun's rays hit
you, giving you strength of conviction. And Thursday is
Jupiter's day, which holds over self-improvement and luck.

92. C. The waxing moon is the time of growth and change.
Not only do Witches work with lunar energies, but they also
use the strong rays of the sun. The hour of midday catches
the extra strength of the rays of the active sun. Sunday is the
sun's day, which holds for magical work on success, career,
finances, and advancement. This is, of course, assuming that
you already have (or soon will) put forth your resumé or
asked your boss for more money!

93. A. The full moon is for general workings and connecting with the Great Mother in her fullness. Twilight is a magical time of introspection, as the lines blur between the realities of the day and night and the moon climbs over the horizon. Monday is the moon's day, which holds over emotions and imagination and dreams.

94. B. A waxing moon is for bringing things to fruition and manifestation. Dawn, for a new beginning. And Friday is the day of Freya—Goddess of love and relationships.

TOTAL YOUR POINTS
Chapter 4, section 6: Crafting the Art of Magical Change

_____ Total number of questions 88–94 answered correctly

Multiply the total number of questions 88–94 answered correctly by 2. This will give you your total number of points for chapter 4, section 6:

_____ X 2 = _____

Total number of questions   Total score, chapter 4,
88–94 answered correctly   section 6

Total possible points for chapter 4, section 6=14

SECTION 7

Working Magic

Questions 95 through 102 are worth 1 point each!

95. A. An iron poker is heated until hot and inserted into the cream. This would stop the Witch who was affecting it by burning him or her and breaking concentration. After the poker was removed, the butter could then be churned.

96. C. An alrum was made by tying together two rowan twigs

of equal length with red thread, forming a solar cross. This was hung for good luck and protection from angry fey folk.

97. A. The Yule log was said to have magical properties. A piece of it was saved to protect the home from lightning strikes.

98. A. Crossing the poker and tongs before the hearth.

99. B. Directly after breaking it, you must turn counterclockwise three times.

100. A. East to west.

101. B. A rope of garlic or onions.

102. C. Salt.

 ## TOTAL YOUR POINTS
Chapter 4, section 7: Working Magic

_____ Total number of questions 95–102 answered correctly

Total possible points for chapter 4, section 7 = 8

TOTALING CHAPTER 4

Add together your final scores from each section in chapter 4:

_____ Chapter 4, section 1—Working Magic
+ _____ Chapter 4, section 2—Hitting the "C" Notes
+ _____ Chapter 4, section 3—Magical Scripts
+ _____ Chapter 4, section 4A—Working with Herbs—Medicinal
+ _____ Chapter 4, section 4B—Working with Herbs—Magical
+ _____ Chapter 4, section 5—Timing Is Everything
+ _____ Chapter 4, section 6—Crafting the Art of Magical Change
+ _____ Chapter 4, section 7—Working Magic

= ☐ Grand total for chapter 4

This is the number you will carry forward to the end of the book!

Total possible points for chapter 4 = 216

5

Unraveling Entrails
The Art of Divination

Will he love me? Is she faithful? Will I get a job? When will money come my way? Where should I go? What should I do? Next to healing, the art of divination has been one of the major trades of a Witch. People want a glimpse into the future to see how their lives will play out and, if possible, to avoid negative outcomes. Since humans have been asking the questions, there have been those who sought ways to answer them. Methods for tapping into hidden knowledge have varied from culture to culture, century to century. Some divination methods that were very popular in ancient times are considered archaic, even disgusting, in our modern world, while others are still very much in use. As our technology, science, and culture evolve, more ways of reaching into the future are developed. Today it is not unusual for folks to turn on their computers to get their daily Web-based divination reading!

SECTION 1

Gazing Into the Future—General Knowledge

1. The art of divination is based upon the assumption that
    a. the diviner has supermagical powers

    b. objects and symbols are independent sources of psychic power

    c. there are links among humans, objects, and the forces found in Nature

    d. divination tools are magical entities

2. Divinatory information is obtained through the reading of
    a. signs in Nature
    b. divination tools (Tarot, et cetera)
    c. omens
    d. all of the above

3. Divination tells the reader
    a. the likely course of events
    b. the actual events that will occur
    c. only past events
    d. where the money is hidden

4. The average Witch is competent in how many forms of divination?
    a. one
    b. three
    c. six
    d. unlimited

5. During medieval times, a cunning person would most often use divination for what purpose?
    a. for healing work
    b. for love magic
    c. to glimpse future events
    d. to determine the identity of a Witch

6. To scry something is
    a. picking up images from holding a personal object
    b. the act of allowing a spirit to use your hand to write a message
    c. concentrating on an object until visions appear
    d. finding symbolic meanings in traffic patterns

7. Which of the following *can't* be used for scrying?

   a. black mirror
   b. french fries
   c. cauldron of water
   d. they can all be used

8. Dowsing requires which tool?
   a. a pendulum
   b. a pool
   c. a rod
   d. either a or c

9. Dowsing is used to
   a. find things
   b. foretell the future
   c. find water
   d. all of the above

10. This form of divination was favored by the ancient Romans:
    a. extispicy
    b. augury
    c. alomancy
    d. haruspicy

11. Picking up images, vibrations, and feelings from objects such as jewelry, clothing, or photographs is called
    a. lychnomancy
    b. psychometry
    c. oneiromancy
    d. onychomancy

12. This is one of the oldest forms of divination in China, dating back more than a thousand years. The divination results, along with the question, were often written down, providing historians and anthropologists with unique insights into the concerns and interests of the ancient Chinese:
    a. oracle bones
    b. I Ching
    c. astrology
    d. Feng Shui

13. Based on Pythagoras's theory that "the world is built upon the power of numbers," this method ascribes value to birth dates and each letter in the alphabet to gain insights into a person's future:
    a. astragalomancy
    b. lithomancy
    c. sortilege
    d. numerology

Mix and Match Mancys

14. Match up each lettered term with its numbered divination definition or technique listed below (1 point per match):

    a. aleuromancy   _____
    b. crystallomancy   _____
    c. chiromancy   _____
    d. alomancy   _____
    e. haruspicy   _____
    f. aeromancy   _____
    g. extispicy   _____
    h. cartomancy   _____
    i. bibliomancy   _____
    j. tasseomancy   _____
    k. sortilege   _____
    l. amniomancy   _____
    m. ceromancy   _____
    n. apantomancy   _____

1. reading tea leaves

2. any divination technique in which objects are cast and you read the pattern they fall in

3. study of the liver and entrails of sacrificed animals

4. this is, literally, "unraveling entrails"

5. reading the lines on a person's hands

6. reading the pattern of molten wax poured into cool water

7. using cards to foretell the future

8. using a sentence or passage picked at random from a book

9. reading the way general clutter is lying

10. predicting an infant's future by reading the caul or afterbirth

11. reading the patterns that salt makes when sprinkled on the floor

12. the predecessor to Chinese fortune cookies

13. divining through the use of the element of air (clouds, sky, weather, and so forth)

14. divination using a crystal ball

SECTION 2

Reading Between the Lines—Palmistry

15. The lines on your hands
   a. are set at birth
   b. change very little as you age
   c. change somewhat with your life
   d. change greatly every year

16. If you're *right*-handed, your _____ hand indicates what you were born with, while your _____ is what you've done with your life. If you're *left*-handed, your _____ hand indicates what you were born with, while your _____ is what you've done with your life.
   a. right; left; left; right
   b. left; right; right; left
   c. right; left; right; left
   d. left; right; left; right

17. The first thing to note when reading a hand is
   a. the shape of the fingers

b. the size of the thumb and palm
c. the shape of the hand
d. the life line

18. If the lines on your hands are deep and clear, then you are apt to be a _____ personality, but if they are faint you can expect _____ .
    a. strong; shallowness
    b. jaded; psychic attunement
    c. forceful; confused
    d. worried; carefree

19. The major line on the palm, and the only one from which time can be approximated, is the
    a. life line
    b. head line
    c. heart line
    d. line of fate

20. The head line indicates
    a. spiritual depth
    b. emotional stability
    c. intelligence
    d. financial gains

21. I have a very long and deep heart line. You would probably tell me
    a. that I have lived a sorrowful life
    b. that I have lived a very joyful life
    c. that I have lived a turbulent life
    d. that I have lived an emotional life

22. I only have one line where my heart and head lines are supposed to be. What does this tell you?
    a. that I'm not very intelligent
    b. that I'm an emotionally distant personality
    c. that my head and my heart are entwined, with a balance formed between the two
    d. that I am an unbalanced personality, capable of genius thought but no emotional control

23. An island on the life line is an indication of
    a. conflicts
    b. ill health
    c. good fortune
    d. nothing, as long as it isn't broken

24. I've got a clear line descending from my middle finger down
    the length of my palm. This is called the
    a. line of Mars
    b. line of Venus
    c. marriage line
    d. line of fate

25. If this symbol appears on the mount of the moon, then you
    will have a natural talent for the occult:
    a. a star
    b. a triangle
    c. a cross
    d. a circle

Lines, Fingers, and Mounts

26. Identify the lines, fingers, and mounts (1 point per correct
    match):

    1. Jupiter finger
    2. mount of Venus
    3. heart line
    4. life line
    5. Saturn finger
    6. head line
    7. Mercury finger
    8. mount of the moon
    9. finger of Apollo
    10. plain of Mars

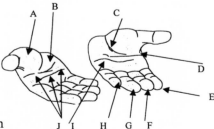

SECTION 3

The Magical Runes

27. One of the oldest forms of runic alphabets is the
    a. Danish
    b. Norse
    c. Germanic
    d. English

28. Runes were originally comprised of _____ symbols, which were then reduced to _____ runes by the Scandinavian peoples in the eight century.
    a. twelve; ten
    b. eighteen; twelve
    c. twenty-four; sixteen
    d. forty-six; thirty-two

29. Collectively, the runes are called the
    a. futhark
    b. aettir
    c. Eddas
    d. mystical doodles

30. The letters are divided into three groups, each group called an
    a. futhark
    b. aettir
    c. suit
    d. triad

31. If you're making a talisman to increase your wealth, which of the following Germanic Runes would be a good sigil to include?

a. ᚠ feoh   b. ᚦ thorn   c. ᚨ os   d. ᚺ hoel

32. If you're making a talisman for safety while traveling, which of the following Germanic Runes would be a good sigil to use?

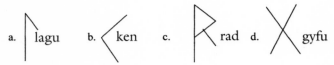

a. lagu   b. ken   c. rad d. gyfu

33. Runes for divinatory purposes can be made out of
    a. wood
    b. stone
    c. paper
    d. anything

34. When cast for a divinatory reading, runes will fall in one of _____ positions.
    a. two
    b. three
    c. four
    d. six

35. A _____ is made by combining multiple runes into one image.
    a. monogram
    b. sigil
    c. gothi mark
    d. hex sign

SECTION 4

Reaching for the Stars—Astrology

36. How many houses are there in the Zodiac?
    a. twelve
    b. ten
    c. eight
    d. 360

37. What information is required to complete a natal chart?
    a. hour of birth, hospital name
    b. parents' names, address, and telephone number
    c. date, time, and location of birth
    d. name of hospital and number of hours the mother was in labor

38. What is a solar return?
    a. summer solstice
    b. Yule
    c. when the sun reaches the same degree it was at when you were born
    d. all of the above

39. I'm empathetic, intuitive, domestic, and a pack rat. What sign am I?
    a. Capricorn
    b. Cancer
    c. Pisces
    d. Virgo

40. In astrology, a house is
    a. a section of the chart with only one Zodiac sign in it
    b. a building with four walls and a roof
    c. a particular grouping of signs within an individual's astrological chart
    d. a mathematical division of the sky

41. Which of the following is *not* an aspect?
    a. trine
    b. conjunction
    c. square
    d. succedent

42. Of the following, which is *not* a water sign?
    a. Cancer
    b. Aquarius
    c. Scorpio
    d. Pisces

43. Of the following, which is a *fixed* sign?
    a. Aries
    b. Sagittarius
    c. Capricorn
    d. Scorpio

44. Of the following, which is a *cardinal* sign?
    a. Cancer
    b. Taurus
    c. Virgo
    d. Gemini

45. When you're looking for information on job and career, which houses should you look at?
    a. first and third
    b. seventh and twelfth
    c. fourth and eleventh
    d. sixth and tenth

46. Conjunction is to zero degrees as_____is to_____.
    a. trine; 120 degrees
    b. square; 45 degrees
    c. opposition; 72 degrees
    d. quintile; 10 degrees

47. To know about someone's love relationships, which planets would you look to?
    a. moon and sun
    b. Neptune and Uranus
    c. moon and Venus
    d. Venus and Mars

48. When two planets are said to be in opposition, it means that they are
    a. 120 degrees apart
    b. ninety degrees apart
    c. 180 degrees apart
    d. five degrees apart

49. Conjunctions are when two planets are
    a. on opposite sides of the chart

b. within the same house

c. within five degrees of each other

d. within the same sign

50. I've had a very easy life; I'm lazy, and everything just comes to me. What aspect predominates within my chart?
    a. square
    b. conjunct
    c. trine
    d. sextile

51. Life has been a series of challenges and obstacles with lessons to be learned. What aspect predominates within my chart?
    a. square
    b. conjunct
    c. trine
    d. sextile

52. Your ascendant is
    a. the time of your birth
    b. the location of your birth
    c. the planets on the horizon at the time of your birth
    d. the sign of the Zodiac on the horizon at the time of your birth

53. In an equal house system, I was born with a Libra sun. I just turned thirty-one. My progressed sun is in
    a. Scorpio
    b. Libra
    c. Leo
    d. Virgo

54. I'm getting married and I need to pick a day. I would want most of my planets in my _____ houses.
    a. fixed
    b. succedent
    c. cadent
    d. angular

55. This book helps the astrologer figure out the positions of the planets:
    a. ephemeris
    b. dictionary
    c. *Linda Goodman's Sun Signs*
    d. *The New Astrology* by White

Mix and Match Sun Signs

56. Match the astrology sun signs with their annual dates (1 point per correct match):

a.	Cancer	_____	1. July 23–August 21
b.	Aquarius	_____	2. November 22–December 21
c.	Gemini	_____	3. April 20–May 19
d.	Libra	_____	4. June 21–July 22
e.	Aries	_____	5. December 22–January 20
f.	Capricorn	_____	6. February 20–March 20
g.	Scorpio	_____	7. March 21–April 19
h.	Sagittarius	_____	8. October 23–November 21
i.	Leo	_____	9. May 20–June 20
j.	Pisces	_____	10. September 23–October 22
k.	Taurus	_____	11. January 21–February 19
l.	Virgo	_____	12. August 22–September 22

Planetary Symbols

57. Match each planet with its symbol (1 point per correct match):

a.	Mars	_____	1.	♃
b.	Venus	_____	2.	♅
c.	Mercury	_____	3.	☉
d.	moon	_____	4.	♆
e.	sun	_____	5.	♂

f.	Pluto	_____	6. ♀
g.	Jupiter	_____	7. ☉
h.	Saturn	_____	8. ☿
i.	Uranus	_____	9. ♀
j.	Neptune	_____	10. ♄

SECTION 5

It's in the Cards—The Tarot

58. A standard deck of Tarot cards consists of how many cards?
    a. twenty-four
    b. fifty-four
    c. seventy-eight
    d. eighty-four

59. The earliest-known reference to cards dates back to
    a. Switzerland, fourteenth century C.E.
    b. Egypt, unknown
    c. Germany, fourth century B.C.E.
    d. India, twelfth century B.C.E.

60. The standard Tarot deck appears to have been descended from an Italian pack known as the
    a. Tarot des Bohemiens
    b. Rider-Waite
    c. Venetian Tarot
    d. Thoth

61. What image was removed from the original Marseilles Tarot under pressure?
    a. the Witch
    b. the Jew
    c. the Horned God
    d. the Papese

62. The four original suits of the Tarot are the
    a. Rock, Paper, Scissors, Water
    b. Earth, Air, Fire, Water

c. Coins, Batons, Cups, Swords
d. Nobility, Peasants, Clergy, Merchants

63. The cards referred to as the trump cards are the
    a. court cards—King, Queen, Knight, Page
    b. the Major Arcana
    c. the Minor Arcana
    d. the term *trump* is used only in playing cards

64. In 1856, Eliphas Lévi suggested a connection between the
    Tarot and
    a. Masonic knowledge
    b. Kabbalistic Tree of Life
    c. alchemic mysteries
    d. lost city of Atlantis

65. The greatest influence on both the images and definitions of
    the Tarot comes from
    a. Golden Dawn
    b. Arthur Waite
    c. Rosicrucians
    d. Masons

66. There have been various forms of Tarot decks printed since
    the 1800s, but the one that set the modern standard is the
    a. Thoth
    b. Mystères de l'Horoscope
    c. Rider-Waite
    d. Marseilles

67. Who was the artist for the Rider-Waite deck?
    a. Lady Frieda Harris
    b. Pamela Colman Smith
    c. Arthur Waite
    d. Pamela Rider

68. Of the following artists, who has not created a Tarot deck?
    a. Salvador Dali
    b. Andy Warhol

    c. Bonifacio Bembo
    d. David Palladini

69. The person for whom a reading is being done is referred to as the
    a. querent
    b. subject
    c. victim
    d. client

70. The significator is the
    a. the Tarotist
    b. card representing the question
    c. card representing the questioner
    d. card representing the problem at hand

71. The most often used Tarot spread is called the
    a. Arch or Horseshoe
    b. Celtic Cross
    c. Tree of Life
    d. Wheel of Fortune

72. I'm doing a reading concerning difficulties in your life. I draw the Five of Wands as the card indicating the heart of the matter. This card tells me that
    a. you're having difficulties choosing a lover among multiple possible partners
    b. the problem lies with difficulties managing money
    c. you've won a battle but feel guilty about the outcome
    d. the struggle is over conflicting opinions and power plays among friends or coworkers.

73. I just came home to find my presumed faithful lover in bed with someone else! Of the following, which card would best represent this current situation?
    a. the Tower
    b. the Lovers
    c. Justice
    d. the Devil

74. The Death card in a reading means
    a. that the questioner will die in the next year
    b. that someone close to the questioner will die in the next month
    c. the ending and transformation of a situation
    d. the ending of a situation

75. What does it indicate if all four Aces appear in a reading?
    a. a bad sign—it means energies are in conflict
    b. a good sign—it strengthens the meaning of the reading
    c. a bad sign—hard decisions will need to be made
    d. a good sign—prizes and honor will come soon

76. If a reading is done and the majority of the cards are Cups, what does this indicate?
    a. the focus of the reading is relationships and human connections
    b. the focus of the reading is work and prosperity
    c. the focus of the reading is struggles and conflicts
    d. the focus of the reading is growth and development

Answers to Chapter 5

Unless otherwise stated, give yourself *2 points for each correct answer.* At the end of the chapter, add together your total points from each section to get your final score for the chapter. This number will be carried forward to the end of the book for a final tally!

SECTION 1

Gazing Into the Future

1. C. Divination is the art of predicting the future. It is based on the assumption that there are links among humans, ob-

jects, and the forces of Nature; if we can learn to read these links, we can predict these natural occurrences.

2. D. All of the above and much, much more!

3. A. Divination will tell you the likely course of events at the time of the reading. The future may change based upon choice. For example, I do a reading for a couple concerning their relationship. Each sign that I see shows nothing but trouble for them. The couple now have a choice. They can ignore the reading and let the future unfold as it will. They can break up, ending the question and the problem. Or they can begin to work on their potential issues, thereby possibly averting the difficult times. The choice is theirs!

4. A. The average Witch is familiar with many different forms of divination, is competent in a couple, but usually favors one. Each form is an art and a skill. Not many artists excel in all media; they usually prefer to work with one, such as painting over sculpture or pottery over stained glass.

5. D. People were very concerned about Witches during medieval times. When I say *Witch,* I mean those individuals said to practice malicious magic in secret, harming property and health. Most clients of the cunning person wanted to know who was responsible for their string of bad luck. They also wanted charms that would propel the bad magic back to the person responsible and protect against further harm.

6. C. Scrying is an ancient art of seeing the future. Using an object, preferably one with a reflective or shiny surface, the clairvoyant focuses upon it, allowing all else to disappear to enter into a trance state. Visions then begin to form on the surface.

7. D. Black mirrors, glass balls, water in a black cauldron, or something with a reflective surface is usually suggested, but in actuality you can scry *anything.* You'd be amazed at what a pizza can tell you!

8. D. Either a pendulum or a rod. Some traditions prefer rods that are made from a hazel twig, but in general it can be constructed from any material.

9. D. Although those who practice dowsing are sometimes called "water Witches," finding underground streams is just one of the tasks of dowsing. Using a pendulum or dowsing rod, *anything* can be located—from lost people to answers to questions and locations on a map.

10. B. Augury is the interpretation of the flight patterns of birds. It is one of the oldest-known and most favored methods of Roman divination. You can find the definitions to the other words listed in "Mix and Match Mancys."

11. B. When a missing person's case becomes difficult, the police will occasionally turn to a medium for help. Using a personal possession or a photo of the subject, the medium will use psychometry to create a connection with the missing for the purpose of finding clues to reveal the location of the missing.

    For Your Learning Enjoyment: Onychomancy is a subset of chiromancy that focuses on the fingernails. Oneiromancy is dream interpretation. Lychnomancy uses the flame from a candle or lamp for scrying.

12. A. Oracle bones was the Chinese method of taking a piece of bone and touching it with a very hot poker. The heat would create cracks on the bone, which were then read. The question was often inscribed on one side of the bone, and the answer on the other to keep for later confirmation. What is amazing is that some of these oracle bones, with their questions and interpretations, have survived to the present day, giving archaeologists and historians a unique look into the minds of the Chinese people more than a thousand years ago!

13. D. Any number can be reduced to a single digit, and each number has certain energies or powers associated with it—

this is the concept behind numerology. Adding your birthday together will give you a single number. This knowledge can then help you find your place in the world. For example: January 20, 1993 = 1 + 2 + 0 + 1 + 9 + 9 + 3 = 19 = 1 + 9 = 10 = 1 + 0 = 1. Those people associated with the number 1 have strong leadership capabilities. They should seek out jobs and situations that will use this skill. In addition, each letter of the alphabet also has a corresponding number from 1 to 9. The letters within your birth name can be added together to give yet another view of your potential.

For Your Learning Enjoyment: Astragalomancy is sortilege using knucklebones. Lithomancy uses stones; sortilege is any divinitory technique in which objects are cast and you read the patterns.

For More Information: Numerology: the Complete Guide by Matthew Oliver Goodwin (Newcastle, 1981).

Mix & Match Mancys

14. Match up each term with its divination definition or divinatory techniques (1 point per match):

a. aleuromancy ___12___ The predecessor to Chinese fortune cookies. The ancient Greeks would insert small pieces of paper into flour balls, which were then offered to people as a means to tell fortunes. The Victorians would bake a coin into a Christmas pudding to give luck to the one whose serving winds up containing the coin.

b. crystallomancy___14___ Divination using a crystal ball.

c. chiromancy ___5___ Reading the lines on a person's hands. This is also known as palmistry.

d. alomancy   _11_   A form of sortilege in which salt is sprinkled on the floor and the patterns created are read.

e. haruspicy   _3_   This is the ancient art of reading entrails, especially the liver, to divine the future or diagnose illness.

f. aeromancy   _13_   Divining through the use of elements found of or in air, such as clouds, breezes, or the weather.

g. extispicy   _4_   This is, literally, "unraveling entrails." Extispicy is divination through the examination of entrails from sacrificial animals.

h. cartomancy   _7_   Using cards to foretell the future. Any kind of cards, from Tarot to playing cards, can be used for divination purposes. My favorite "deck" is a collection of postcards that I've been amassing over the last ten years.

i. bibliomancy   _8_   Using a sentence or passage picked at random from a book.

j. tasseomancy   _1_   The reading of tea leaves has been a popular form of divination for many years. Unstrained tea is poured into a cup and drunk, leaving a bit of liquid on the bottom. The cup is rotated, allowing the herbs to coat the inside of the cup, then inverted onto a saucer to remove the last bit of liquid. The diviner interprets the various shapes and forms created by the remaining leaves.

k. sortilege   _2_   Any divination technique in which objects are cast and you read the pattern they fall in.

l. amniomancy   _10_   Predicting an infant's future by reading the caul or afterbirth.

m. ceromancy   _6_   Reading the pattern molten wax makes when poured into cool water.

n. apantomancy   _9_   Reading the way general clutter is lying.

_____Total number of correct matches in question 14: the Fancy Mancys

TOTAL YOUR POINTS
Chapter 5, section 1: Gazing Into the Future

_____ Total number of questions 1–13 answered correctly

Multiply the total number of questions 1–13 answered correctly by 2:

_____ X 2 = _____
Total number of questions 1–13   Total 2-point questions,
answered correctly   chapter 5, section 1

_____ Total number of 1-point matches, question 14.

Add together your 2-point total with your 1-point total:

_____ + _____ = _____
1-point total,   2-point total,   Total score, chapter
question 14   questions 1–13   5, section 1

Total possible points for chapter 5, section 1 = 40

SECTION 2
Reading Between the Lines—Palmistry

15. C. The lines on your hands change as you age, reflecting your life lessons experienced and giving you outlines for your possible future.

16. B. If you're *right*-handed, your left hand indicates what you came into this life with, while your right indicates what you've done with it. If you're *left*-handed, this is reversed.

17. C. Because the shape of the hand is the base from which a palmist works, it is the first thing that is looked at. Different-sized hands indicate different things about a person. For example, a short square hand will belong to someone who is practical and enjoys doing physical things, while a long and thin hand implies a tendency toward the artistic.

18. A. A strong line indicates a strong personality, someone who isn't afraid to live life with all its ups and downs. Those who have faint lines tend to be more shallow or have become jaded with life.

19. A. The life line is the major line of the palm. It is the only line from which time can be approximated. According to Peter West in his book *Life Lines: An Introduction to Palmistry* (Aquarian Press, 1981), you measure time by creating an imaginary line straight down from the index finger to the life line. This is equal to about the first ten years of life. For age twenty, draw another imaginary line from the in-between part of your index and middle fingers down to the life line. Thirty-five is the imaginary line from the middle of your middle finger to your life line. The space between these last two markers will give you the time distance per fifteen years. You can use this measurement to calculate the remainder of your line.

20. C. The head line is your intellect. It should always be looked at in connection with the heart line, because they balance each other. A strong line shows deep intelligence.

21. D. The depth of the heart line indicates the depth of emotions. Those with a long and deep line feel deeply, both the good and the bad in their lives.

22. C. Those with a combined head and heart line are interesting. It means that their emotions and their intellect are in balance; one does not lead the other in making decisions.

23. B. An island is an indication of ill health. The size and length can tell you approximately how long the illness will last. A break in the head line can be a sign of potential head trauma!

24. D. Not everyone has a line of fate. For those who do, the deeper and longer it is, the more good fortune will come. Those who have a line from their wrist all the way to their middle finger without a break have the luck of the Lady; everything seems to go their way without effort. Those whose line ends at their head or their heart lines will find their head or their heart gets in the way of good fortune. Those who do not have a line of fate will need to work hard for what they want in life.

25. B. A triangle on the mount of the moon indicates a natural talent for psychic and occult mysteries.

Lines, Fingers, and Mounts

26. Identify these lines, fingers, and mounts (1 point per correct match):
    1. Jupiter finger   = E, for executive abilities, confidence, ambition, pride.
    2. mount of Venus   = A, warmth and kindness. Many small lines crossing this mount indicates a person who worries a lot.
    3. heart line   = I.
    4. life line   = C.

  5. Saturn finger   = F, nature and sociability.
  6. head line   = D.
  7. Mercury finger   = H, cleverness, communication, business ability.
  8. mount of the moon   = B, psychic development and imagination.
  9. finger of Apollo   = G, art and beauty.
 10. plain of Mars   = J, there are actually three areas that make up the plain of Mars: the center of the palm and to the right and left of it. A full and solid plain indicates interaction with the world and worldly affairs.

_____ Total number of correct matches in question 26, Lines, Fingers, and Mounts

For More Information: Life Lines: An Introduction to Palmistry by Peter West (Aquarian Press, 1981).

TOTAL YOUR POINTS
Chapter 5, section 2: Palmistry

_____ Total number of 2-point questions, numbers 15–25 answered correctly

Multiply your total number of questions 15–25 answered correctly by 2:

_____ X 2 = _____
Total number of 2-point   Total score 2-point questions,
questions 15–25   chapter 5, section 3

_____ Total Number of 1-point matches, question 26

Add together your 2-point question total with your 1-point question total:

_____ + _____ = _____

1-point total,   2-point total,   Total score, chapter 5,
question 26   questions 15–25   section 2

Total possible points for chapter 5, section 2 = 32

SECTION 3
The Magical Runes

27. C. Germanic peoples were using runes in the second century C.E. Scandinavian and Icelandic peoples picked them up in the twelfth century C.E. English, or Anglo-Saxon, was used in Britain somewhere between the fifth and twelfth centuries C.E.

28. C. The Germanic Runes consisted of twenty-four. The Norse reduced this number to sixteen by allowing some runes to stand for more than one letter. The Asatru, a modern reconstructionist religion, uses the original twenty-four runes.

29. A. Collectively, the runes are called the futhark. This name comes from the first six letters of the runes: *f, u, th, a, r,* and *k.*
    For Your Learning Enjoyment: The prose and poetic Eddas are the texts that recorded the ancient oral traditions of Norse ritual and mythology.

30. B. The letters are divided into three groups of eight, with each group called an aettir or "family." Each aettir is attributed to a particular deity: Freya, Heimdall, or Tiwaz.

31. A. Feoh represents property and wealth.
    For Your Learning Enjoyment: Thorn refers to the Frost Giants and demons who threaten the Gods. It is a rune of attack and overcoming fears. Os is a great rune to use if you

do any public speaking, because it has the power of invocation and inspiration. Hoel represents disruption and potential loss.

32. C. Rad is good for safe travel.
   For Your Learning Enjoyment: Lagu may be helpful if you
   are bringing a whole bunch of people with you—this is the
   rune for community. Lagu can also help when you're trying
   to find a lover. Ken might aid you in figuring out which direction to go, because this rune reveals hidden knowledge.
   Gyfu is a symbol of sacrifice. Not something I would want
   on a talisman for travel!

33. D. Anything, although traditionally runes were carved on
   pieces of wood or twigs.

34. C. Four positions: face-up upright, face-up reversed, facedown upright, facedown reversed.

35. A. A monogram combines multiple runes into one single
   image for magical purposes. Because runes are made up of
   lines, it is easy to combine them, creating a new form. For
   example, for success in a new business, combine ur (taking
   risk for possible growth) and ger (action leading to good results, success, or rewards):

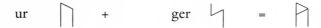

*For More Information: Using the Runes: A Comprehensive Intro-
duction to the Art of Runecraft* by D. Jason Cooper (Aquarian
Press, 1987). *Runelore: A Handbook of Esoteric Runology* by Edred
Thorsson (Samuel Weiser, 1987).

TOTAL YOUR POINTS
Chapter 5, section 3: The Magical Runes

_____ Total number of questions 27–35 answered correctly

Multiply the total number of questions 27–35 answered correctly by 2. This will give you your total number of points for chapter 5, section 3:

_____ X 2 = _____
Total number of questions 27–35   Total score, chapter 5,
answered correctly   section 3

Total possible points, chapter 5, section 3 = 18

SECTION 4
Reaching for the Stars—Astrology

36. A. There are twelve houses in the Zodiac.

37. C. In order to find our where the planets, and hence influencing energies, were at the time of birth, you need to fix the location, the time, and the date.

38. C. The solar return is when the sun reaches the same degree it was at when you were born, which is not always the same as your birthday.

39. B. Oriented toward home, hearth, family, memories, intuitive, sensitive—these are just some of the attributes of the typical moonchild, also known as Cancerian.
    For Your Learning Enjoyment: Capricorns are ambitious and are materially or power-oriented. They enjoy figuring out the rules of the game of life, so they can use them to their advantage. Pisceans, on the other hand, sees the rules but can't figure out why anyone would bother using a rulebook. They are sensitive and, at times, vague. Virgos read the rulebook because they're afraid that if they don't, they might accidentally break one! Tidy and conservative, they have a tendency to be analytical.

40. D. A house is the mathematical division of the sky based on the exact spot where you were born. As the sun moves, it passes through twelve houses and twelve different constella-

tions. There are three groups of four houses, each house sharing common characteristics.

41. D. When two planets are a certain number of degrees from each other, they are said to be in aspect. The type of aspect depends on the number of degrees. A succedent is one of the three groupings of houses that share certain characteristics—in this case the second, fifth, eighth, and eleventh. Angular houses are the first, fourth, seventh, and tenth. Cadent houses are the third, sixth, ninth, and twelfth.

42. B. Aquarius, depicted as the water carrier, is actually an air sign.

43. D. A fixed sign is set in the middle month of each season.

44. A. A cardinal sign falls at the beginning month of each season. Cancer marks the beginning of the summer.

45. D. The sixth house is the house that shows your work and your health, while the tenth house indicates profession, business, and social activities.

46. A. Trine is to 120 degrees.

47. D. The planets Venus and Mars are much like their namesakes. Venus rules passions and relationships, while Mars involves more animalistic desires and sexual energies.

48. C. Two planets that are 180 degrees apart. This is the widest possible aspect. It shows challenges due to opposing energies, but if balance is found, they can complement each other.

49. C. Two planets that are within five degrees of each other are said to be conjunct. It adds intensity to the sign and house in which they are found. A conjunction could be favorable or provide challenges, depending upon which planets are conjunct. A group of three or more planets in conjunction with each other is called a stellium.

50. C. A trine is when two planets are within 120 degrees of each other. A trine is usually favorable. It permits easy inter-action and flow among the energies of the planets. The neg-ative aspect of trines is that because life comes easy, there may be a tendency not to seek out challenges and become lazy. A grand trine is three planets, all in the same element, that are 120 degrees apart.

51. A. Those who have planets square—two or three are lo-cated ninety degrees apart—unfortunately have a lot of life lessons to learn. The difficulties will depend on whether the square is cardinal, fixed, or mutable.

52. D. Your ascendant is the sign on the horizon at the time of your birth.

53. A. Scorpio. There are different techniques on how to di-vide the sky into twelve houses. Because a complete circle is 360 degrees, the simplest method is to divide it evenly into 30 degrees per house. An equal house has thirty degree in each house. A progression is a way of moving the planets one day for each year to see how they relate to each other. The sun takes about a year to move a degree. So thirty-one years will move your sun into the next house.

54. D. Angular houses correspond to the cardinal signs. They are the first, which holds the energies of the self and new be-ginnings; the fourth, which is for the home and family; the seventh, for marriage and partnerships; and the tenth, which is your standing in your community. All are positive for a wedding ceremony.

55. A. An ephemeris is a book listing the positions of the plan-ets at different times. A table of houses is a tool. This one gives the correlations of the planets in regard to location.

Mix and Match Sun Signs

56. Match the sun signs with their annual dates (1 point per match):

a.	Cancer	___4___	June 21–July 22
b.	Aquarius	___11___	January 21–February 19
c.	Gemini	___9___	May 20–June 20
d.	Libra	___10___	September 23–October 22
e.	Aries	___7___	March 21–April 19
f.	Capricorn	___5___	December 22–January 20
g.	Scorpio	___8___	October 23–November 21
h.	Sagittarius	___2___	November 22–December 21
i.	Leo	___1___	July 23–August 21
j.	Pisces	___6___	February 20–March 20
k.	Taurus	___3___	April 20–May 19
l.	Virgo	___12___	August 22–September 22

_____ Total number of matches in question 56: Mix and Match Sun Signs

Planetary Symbols

57.   Match each planet with its symbol (1 point per match):

a.	Mars	___5___	♂
b.	Venus	___9___	♀
c.	Mercury	___8___	☿
d.	moon	___7___	⊙
e.	sun	___3___	☉
f.	Pluto	___6___	♀
g.	Jupiter	___1___	♃
h.	Saturn	___10___	♄
i.	Uranus	___2___	♅
j.	Neptune	___4___	♆

_____ Total number of matches in question 57: Planets and Symbols

For More Information: The Only Way to Learn Astrology, Volume 1: Basic Principles by Marion D. March and Joan McEvers (ACS Publications, 1980). *The Only Astrology Book You'll Ever Need* by Joanna Martine Woolfolk (Madison Books, 2001).

TOTAL YOUR POINTS
Chapter 5, section 4: Astrology

_____ Total number of 2-point questions, numbers 36–55, answered correctly

Multiply your total number of questions 36–55 answered correctly by 2:

_____ X 2 = _____
Total number of 2-point   Total score, 2-point questions,
questions 36–55 answered   chapter 5, section 4
correctly

Add together the 1-point questions:

____ Total number of 1-point matches, question 56, Sun Signs
+ ____ Total number of 1-point matches, question 57, Planetary Symbols
= ____ Combined total of 1-point matches, questions 56 and 57

Add together your 2-point question total and your 1-point question total:

_____ + _____ = _____
Total 1-point   Total 2-point   Total score, chap-
questions, 56   questions, 36–55   ter 5, section 4
and 57

Total possible points for chapter 5, section 4 = 62

SECTION 5

It's in the Cards—The Tarot

58. C. The standard deck of Tarot cards consists of seventy-eight cards.

59. A. The first mention of playing cards dates back to a letter written in 1377 C.E. by a monk living in Switzerland. Brother John mentioned a "certain game called the game of cards" but he seemed unsure where it derived from or when. He described what sounds more like what we would think of as a modern pack of cards, not Tarot cards.

60. C. The Venetian Tarot, produced in the 1500s, includes the twenty-two additional cards with some images that are still familiar in modern decks. It is the same as the French pack, Tarot of Marseilles. In fact, the word *Tarot* is a French derivative of the Italian *tarocchi*.

   For Your Learning Enjoyment: *Le Tarot des Bohemiens* or "Tarot of the Gypsies" was a book produced in 1889 by Gerard Encausses, otherwise known as Papus. It combines the Tarot with numerology and the Tree of Life. The Thoth deck was created by Aleister Crowley. The Rider-Waite deck wasn't fashioned until 1910.

61. D. Under pressure from the pope, *La Papese,* otherwise known as the female pope, was removed from the deck and replaced with the image of a woman who stood for faithfulness or constancy. In modern decks, she is the High Priestess.

62. C. These are the more original suits. In modern decks, Pentacles are often substituted for Coins and Wands for Batons. The association of the elements with the suits is a more modern concept. Some Tarotists do theorize that the four suits relate to the four classes of the populace found in medieval times.

63. B. The Major Arcana, the twenty-two specialized cards, are called the trump cards.

64. B. In his book *History of Magic,* Eliphas Lévi, whose real
name was Alphonse Louis Constant, made public his opinion that the cards formed a type of science in the form of hi-
eroglyphics. He was the first one to tie the Kabbalah in with
the Tarot, connecting the trumps with the twenty-two letters of the Hebrew alphabet, the four suits with the four letters used for the name of God, and the ten minor cards of
each suit with the ten aspects of God. While there is no real
evidence for this claim, occultists since then have taken it as
fact or at least continue to use the principles.

65. A. Arthur Waite, Samuel Mathers, and Aleister Crowley,
among many other well-known occultists, were all members
of the Hermetic Order of the Golden Dawn. Using the earlier writings of Eliphas Lévi as its base, the Golden Dawn
went farther by constructing a system that integrated the
Kabbalah, alchemy, astrology, numerology, and magic with
the Tarot. As a teaching order, it passed this system on to
students. Waite joined the Golden Dawn in 1891. It was
these teachings that led him to design the deck as we know
it today.

66. C. Arthur Waite created the "rectified" deck in 1910. It is
also the first Tarot deck to use pictures for the Minor
Arcana! It is from this deck that most modern decks are now
derived. Waite's companion book is titled *The Pictorial Key
to the Tarot.*
     For Your Learning Enjoyment: Aleister Crowley fashioned
the Thoth deck and its guide, *The Book of Thoth.* It is based
on the philosophy of the Temple of the Orient or O.T.O.
Les Mystères de l'Horoscope was designed by Eugene Jacob
and his wife for the use of fortune-telling. The Marseilles
deck is the French deck dating back to the 1500s. While it
has some of the familiar trump card images, it is not the
form used today.

67. B. Pamela Colman Smith and Arthur Waite were both involved with the Golden Dawn. They teamed up to create

the deck, Smith using her artistic talents and insights and Waite's guidance. Lady Frieda Harris designed Crowley's Thoth cards, which embody teachings from his *Book of the Law.*

68. B. As far as I can tell, Andy never illustrated a deck of Tarot cards.

    For Your Learning Enjoyment: Bonifacio Bembo is a famous fifteenth-century artist whose Tarot images and artwork are now museum pieces. David Palladini crafted the Aquarian Tarot. Even modern artist Salvador Dali has offered up his Tarot visions. Just in case you've been dying to know, Fergus Hall was the master behind the James Bond 007 Tarot Cards.

69. A. The querent is the person with the question. This could be the reader him- or herself, or the individual for whom the Tarotist is doing a reading.

70. C. The card representing the querent, or questioner, is called the significator. Some methods assign particular court cards based upon the querent's physical appearance (for example, the Queen of Cups for a younger, light-haired woman). Others suggest that either the reader or the querent locate a card in the deck that "feels right." In the reading, this card is the base upon which the rest of the cards are then placed—or the card can be reinserted in the deck to see where in the reading it best reveals itself.

71. B. The ten-card reading called the Celtic Cross or Grand Cross is one of the most popular styles of reading. It was suggested by Waite for answering specific questions. The layout of the cards, which forms a cross, is uniform, but the interpretation of each position often becomes personalized. The Five Card spread is used for minor questions, or when you're in a hurry. The Tree of Life integrates the Kabbalah positions, and the interactions between them, on the Tree of Life with the Tarot. The Wheel of Fortune is done in a cir-

cular positioning. There are perhaps thousands of variations on Tarot spreads.

72. D. The Five of Wands in the Rider-Waite deck shows five people struggling with each other. Each is dressed differently. None is making eye contact with any others in the group. The ground is bare of growth, and no water is visible. If you look closely, you can see that with only a little bit of effort, their staves could form a pentacle, symbol of earth and manifestation. This is the card for everyone having their own idea of how to accomplish something and not communicating or working well with others. The fiery power plays have torched the ground, leaving nothing useful to grow. Unless other cards indicate differently, I often read this as occurring at work.

73. A. The Tower is the world crashing down—the bursting of the bubble of perceived realities, those things that you believed to be truths, to reveal the actual. It is a coming down to Earth . . . the hard way.

74. C. The Death card, despite its appearance, does not indicate an actual death. It is a card of transformation. It speaks of the natural endings of things, which move into rebirth, the creation of something new, continuously following the cycles of Nature. For this reason, the answer is C and not D. A card of endings with little hope is the Ten of Swords— although even in that card, a sunrise in the background indicates that new possibilities can be fashioned; it's just that they won't be from the current situation. As far as indicating physical death within a reading, some readers look to a combination of the Moon card with either Death or the Ten of Swords. Mathers saw this outcome if the Death card fell between the Nine of Swords and the Three of Swords. Others dislike touching this topic entirely.

75. B. The cards of the same number all share a similar type of energy. The more cards of the same number appear in a

reading, the stronger is the energy reflected within that number. For example, the Aces are the embodiment of the suit they represent. They all represent forms of new possibilities and the development of strengths. The more Aces in a reading, the stronger and more numerous the possibilities.

76. A. Cups, often equated with the element water, reflect matters of the heart: love, relationships, human connections, emotions. Wands hold the attributes of fire: creativity, drive, ambition, home. Swords represent air: the intellect, logic, and conflicts. Pentacles are earth: growth, manifestation, material, work. If the reading is predominantly one suit, it is a clear indication what the focus of the energies in question are!

For More Information: Seventy-Eight Degrees of Wisdom: A Book of Tarot by Rachel Pollack (Thorson Publishing, 1998) or *Learning the Tarot: A Tarot Book for Beginners* by Joan Bunning (Red Wheel/Weiser, 1998).

TOTAL YOUR POINTS
Chapter 5, section 5: The Tarot

_____Total number of questions 58–76, answered correctly

Multiply the total number of questions 58–76 answered correctly by 2. This will give you your total number of points for chapter 5, section 5:

_____ X 2 = _____
Total number of questions 58–76   Total score, chapter 5,
answered correctly   section 5

Total possible points for chapter 5, section 5 = 38

TOTALING CHAPTER 5

Add together your final scores from each section in Chapter 5:

_____ Chapter 5, section 1—Gazing Into the Future
+ _____ Chapter 5, section 2—Palmistry
+ _____ Chapter 5, section 3—The Magical Runes
+ _____ Chapter 5, section 4—Astrology
+ _____ Chapter 5, section 5—The Tarot

= ☐ Grand total for chapter 5

This is the number you will carry forward to the end of the book!

Total possible points for chapter 5 = 190

6

Cerebellum Ceremonium
Ceremonial Magic

Why a chapter on Ceremonial Magic in a book on Wicca? It's because most of Wiccan practices, theories, ritual structure, and symbolism can be traced back to these magical lodges and societies. Ceremonial Magic, and those who practice it, actually have a history traceable back to ancient Greece, and perhaps even earlier! Having some knowledge of the roots and soil from which Wicca grew is important in an understanding of the religion itself. This chapter is an overview of Ceremonial Magic and those aspects that are most frequently seen within Wiccan traditions.

SECTION 1
Brushing the Dust off History

1. These sacred books of mystical wisdom are attributed to Hermes Trismegistus. They date to somewhere between the third century B.C.E. and the first century C.E., and had an enormous impact of the development of Western occultism and magical practices:
   a. Trismegistus Megus
   b. Corpus Hermetica

c. Hermes Corpus Metrus

d. Hermetica Trimetica

2. Nicolas Flammel, a fifteenth-century French alchemist from Germany, was an expert on the Kabbalah. He reportedly found three books that were later translated by S. L. Mathers. These works were a major influence on magicians and occultists, such as Aleister Crowley, and may even have been the basis from which Gerald Gardner derived some of his *Book of Shadows*. The original author was said to have been

a. Mosabra the Mystic

b. Abrameline the Mage

c. Samuel the Sage

d. Saul the Seer

3. Paracelsus was born in 1493. As a philosopher and alchemist, he attempted to unite the spirituality found in Nature with Christian dogma. He saw the cosmos as a single entity, the divine womb of the Mother Earth. It is from Paracelsus that we get the saying

a. so mote it be

b. an if it harm none

c. do what thou wilt

d. as above, so below

4. Written by Agrippa during the sixteenth century, this three-volume book had an enormous effect on the development of Western occult thought:

a. *The Book of the Law*

b. *Magic in Theory and in Practice*

c. *The Magus*

d. *On Occult Philosophy*

5. Ceremonial Magicians of the older occult orders viewed demons as

a. part of evil, Satanic practices

b. silly folk nonsense

c. powerful intelligences who can be summoned and controlled in rituals

    d. powerful and dangerous entities who need to be destroyed

6. As an alchemist, mathematician, and astrologer to Queen Elizabeth I, he is called the "last royal magician." He, along with his partner Edward Kelly, developed the Enochian system of magic, which is a method for summoning spirits and traveling in the astral planes:
    a. Eliphas Lévi
    b. John Dee
    c. Paracelsus
    d. MacGregor Mathers

7. Francis Barrett was an Englishman and novelist in the nineteenth century. He wrote a book titled _____,which included, among many other topics, the concept of natural magic found in stones and herbs, alchemy, numerology, and Ceremonial Magic. The most unusual thing about this book is that it also included _____.
    a. *Magic in Theory and in Practice;* political ravings
    b. *On Occult Practice;* angelic connections
    c. *The Book of Magic;* newspaper articles on magic
    d. *The Magus;* an advertisement seeking students

8. These are handbooks of magic, sometimes referred to as "black books," that are used by students of Ceremonial Magic. Reputedly dating back to ancient sources, they contain instructions on how to conjure demons, details of various rituals, instructions for creating amulets and talismans, and other occult knowledge:
    a. magical manuals
    b. books of shadows
    c. grimoires
    d. diaries

9. Of the following known black books, which is the oldest and most famous?
    a. *Lemegeton*
    b. *Key of Solomon*

c. *Grimoire of Honorius*

d. *The Book of Black Magic and of Pacts*

10. What are "names of power"?
    a. Isis, Astarte, Diana, Hecate
    b. personal names used only during ritual
    c. the names of the hidden masters on the astral planes in Tibet
    d. secret names that are used to invoke or raise energy

11. When Eliphas Lévi attempted to answer the question, "Why does magic work?" in his book *The Dogma and Ritual of High Magic* (1856), his theories made a major impact on the thinking of Magicians and on those who would later be known as modern Witches. The Hermetic Order of the Golden Dawn is based upon his writings. Lévi put forth three laws of magic. They are
    a. power of will, astral light, and the connection between the macro- and the microcosm
    b. the power of Nature, the bending of energy to will, the connection of all
    c. to will, to dare, to know
    d. imagination, action, manifestation

SECTION 2

The Hermetic Order of the Golden Dawn

The original order of this Western occult society was short lived, only from 1888 to 1903, yet its impact on magical practices as we know them today is immeasurable. Many well-known personalities, both occult and popular, were members. The order accepted initiates of both sexes, and was the starting point for a number of other esoteric organizations. Traces of Golden Dawn practices, ritual format, and magical approaches can be found within the majority of Wiccan Traditions. With the resurgence of interest, the Hermetic Order of the Golden Dawn was reconstituted in the early 1980s.

12. The Hermetic Order of the Golden Dawn was the most influential of the Western occult societies in the twentieth century. It was founded in 1887 by
   a. W. R. Woodman
   b. MacGregor Mathers
   c. A. F. A. Woodford
   d. Wynn Westcott

13. The oldest of the Golden Dawn temples was
   a. Osiris
   b. Isis-Urania
   c. Horus
   d. Amen-Ra

14. The Golden Dawn tradition is considered a cross between
   a. Wiccan and Druid practices
   b. alchemic and Kabbalistic practices
   c. Rosicrucian and Masonic practices
   d. Masonic and Christian practices

15. The original Hermetic Order of the Golden Dawn was established in 1888 with these three individual as the "Chiefs" of the secret society. Of the following, who wasn't one of the three?
   a. Wynn Westcott
   b. MacGregor Mathers
   c. A. E. Waite
   d. W. R. Woodman

16. Of the following, who was never a member of the Golden Dawn?
   a. W. B. Yeats
   b. Bram Stoker
   c. Aleister Crowley
   d. Gerald Gardner

17. The Golden Dawn consists of an elaborate hierarchy of grades or degrees. These included _____ orders and _____ degrees or grades.

    a. three; ten
    b. ten; thirty-three
    c. five; thirteen
    d. three; thirty-three

18. The higher grades of the Third Order are
    a. obtained through three days of examination and the agreement of all members to the candidate's acceptability
    b. administrative positions
    c. obtained only after twenty-five years of membership within the society
    d. unobtainable in life

19. Of the following, which Wiccan practice comes out of the Golden Dawn?
    a. elements and color associations
    b. assuming God forms
    c. Watchtowers
    d. all of the above

SECTION 3

Cloaked in Secrecy—Influential Magical Societies

20. The O.T.O. is a German society formed in the Templar tradition. It was founded in 1902 by Freemason Karl Kellner. What do the letters *O.T.O.* stand for?
    a. Ordo Templi Orifice
    b. Official Templar Order
    c. Ordo Templi Orientis
    d. Ordinary Templar Order

21. Along with aspects of Freemasonry and Hermetics, the focus of the O.T.O. is largely on
    a. assuming God forms
    b. Hindu spirituality
    c. Kabbalah
    d. sex magic

22. What was the name of the O.T.O. chapter headed by Aleister Crowley?
    a. Stella Matutina
    b. Alpha et Omega
    c. Roseae Rubeae et Aureae Crucis
    d. Mysteria Mystica Maxima

23. What was the prerequisite for membership into the Rosicrucian Society?
    a. obtaining the secret password from a member
    b. extensive knowledge of alchemic principles
    c. rank of Master Freemason
    d. having the proper contacts and education

24. The ideology of the Rosicrucian Society included
    a. the re-creation of Hermetic texts and rituals
    b. alchemic and Kabbalistic principles applied to ritual format
    c. Gnosticism and Christian doctrine applied to alchemic and esoteric studies
    d. the integration of folk magic with ceremonial magic

25. The Theosophical Society was founded in New York City in 1875 by Helena Petrovna Blavatsky and who?
    a. MacGregor Mathers
    b. H. S. Olcott
    c. W. R. Woodman
    d. Wentworth Little

26. In 1877, Helena Petrovna Blavatsky, founder of the Theosophical Society, published a book that had a major influence on occult thinking and magical societies. It was called
    a. *Foundation of Practical Magic*
    b. *Isis Unveiled*
    c. *The Magus*
    d. *Portable Darkness*

27. He was Aleister Crowley's secretary from 1928 to 1934 and a member of Stella Matutina, a magical order derived from

the Golden Dawn. He wrote numerous books on occultism and, violating his oath of secrecy, published the rituals of the Golden Dawn:

a. Scott Michaelsen

b. Aidan Kelly

c. Jack L. Bracelin

d. Israel Regardie

28. Aleister Crowley was the most controversial occultist of the twentieth century. Allegedly, a being appeared to Crowley in April 1904 and began dictating to him a prose poem called

a. the Portal of Darkness

b. the Charge of the Goddess

c. the Call to Life

d. Liber Al vel Legis

29. The Law of Thelema states

a. do what thou wilt shall be the whole of the law

b. I am what is attained at the end of desire

c. live, laugh, and love

d. you shall honor and obey Crowley

30. In a Masonic Lodge, which direction is considered the "place of darkness"?

a. north

b. east

c. south

d. west

31. Annie Besant (1847–1923) became head of the Theosophical Society upon the death of Colonel H. S. Olcott. She was also influential in forming the _____ , of which Gerald Gardner became a member.

a. Societas Rosicruciana Anglia

b. Rosicrucian Fellowship

c. Stella Matutina

d. British Co-Masons

32. Of the following, which is *not* a Masonic term or practice that can be found in modern Wicca?
    a. So Mote It Be
    b. properly prepared
    c. Craft of the Wise
    d. elemental associations

SECTION 4

Working With Angels—Ceremonial Magic

33. What are the four powers of the Magus?
    a. strength, will, focus, action
    b. belief, focus, action, silence
    c. knowledge, courage, will, silence
    d. truth, courage, belief, force

34. This symbol is worn about the neck of the Magician so that it rests upon the chest:
    a. pentacle
    b. sigil
    c. lamen
    d. sash

35. These two pillars, one black and one white, are philosophical constructs found in the Kabbalah and the Tarot. They are also physical symbols in a ceremonial circle and in a Masonic lodge. They are called _____ and _____ , and they represent _____ and _____, respectively.
    a. Just and Because; justice and fate
    b. Jachin and Boaz; mercy and judgment
    c. John and Baptist; faith and truth
    d. Jupiter and Bacchus; restraint and self-indulgence

36. On which side of the altar is the white pillar?
    a. left
    b. right
    c. east
    d. doesn't matter

37. This is one of the essential Hermetic rituals. It is used to purify the space within the magic circle and to empower the Magician:
    a. Greater Banishing Ritual
    b. Rite of Purification
    c. Lesser Banishing Ritual
    d. Pentacle and the Middle Pillar

38. What is a decagon?
    a. a geometric figure
    b. a sephiroth in the Kabbalah
    c. an elemental focus
    d. a tool for summoning the Gods

39. The following is a symbol of
    a. air
    b. fire
    c. water
    d. earth

40. The following is a symbol of
    a. air
    b. fire
    c. water
    d. earth

41. The following is a symbol of
    a. air
    b. fire
    c. water
    d. earth

42. The following is a symbol of
    a. air
    b. fire
    c. water
    d. earth

43. Of the following archangels, who is *not* invoked in the Lesser Ritual of the Pentagram?

a. Auriel
b. Gabriel
c. Raphael
d. Samuel

44. In the Lesser Ritual of the Pentagram, Michael stands in which position?
    a. before you
    b. behind you
    c. at your right hand
    d. at your left hand

45. What are the alchemical names of the three principles of Nature?
    a. copper, brass, silver
    b. sulfur, mercury, salt
    c. gold, silver, mercury
    d. wood, water, iron

46. The four Kerubs are seen on both the Tarot cards the Wheel of Fortune and the World in the Rider-Waite deck. They are associated with the four elements. Match up the Kerub with its corresponding element (1 point per correct match):

    a. Lion   _____   1. earth
    b. Bull   _____   2. air
    c. Man   _____   3. fire
    d. Eagle   _____   4. water

47. Match up each metal with its corresponding planet in alchemy (1 point per correct match):

    a. lead   _____   1. Mars
    b. tin   _____   2. Venus
    c. iron   _____   3. Jupiter
    d. gold   _____   4. moon
    e. copper/brass   _____   5. Saturn
    f. quicksilver   _____   6. Mercury
    g. silver   _____   7. Sun

SECTION 5

Climbing the Tree of Life—The Kabbalah

The Kabbalah or Qabbalah is also referred to as the Tree of Life. It is an essential part of Jewish mystery tradition. Christian occultists interested in Hermeticism incorporated it into their practices. Arthur Waite of the Golden Dawn integrated the symbolism of the Kabbalah into the modern Tarot. The Kabbalah was also the basis for many of the rites of the Golden Dawn and other mystery orders.

48. How many sephiroth are there?
    a. eight
    b. ten
    c. twelve
    d. fifteen

49. How many paths of wisdom are found on the Tree?
    a. twelve
    b. twenty-two
    c. thirty-two
    d. forty-two

50. How many sephiroth are on the middle pillar?
    a. three
    b. four
    c. five
    d. six

51. How many worlds of the Kabbalah are there?
    a. three
    b. four
    c. ten
    d. twenty-two

52. What do the three pillars of the Kabbalah represent?
    a. severity, mildness, mercy
    b. wisdom, understanding, knowledge
    c. victory, strength, will
    d. birth, age, death

53. Assiah is
    a the female name of God
    b the void or veil
    c the third sephiroth on the right-hand side of the Tree
    d the lowest world of the Kabbalah and represents the physical plane

54. What is the sephiroth between Tiphareth and Kether on the middle pillar?
    a. Malkuth
    b. Da'ath
    c. Yesod
    d. Chokmah

55. Where is the sephiroth "the kingdom" located?
    a. at the top of the Tree
    b. at the bottom of the Tree
    c. at the top right of the Tree
    d. at the top left of the Tree

56. The sephiroth _____ is associated with the element air and is considered the foundation of _____.
    a. Yesod; manifestation
    b. Hod; thought
    c. Geburah; will
    d. Binah; emotion

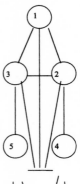

57. Using the figure, match up each numbered sephiroth with its name (1 point per correct match):
    a. Thiphareth ____   f. Geburah ____
    b. Yesod   ____   g. Hod   ____
    c. Chokmah   ____   h. Kether   ____
    d. Netzach   ____   i. Malkuth ____
    e. Chesed   ____   j. Binah   ____

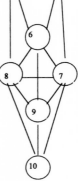

58. Using the same figure as in question 57, match up each sephiroth with its attributes (1 point per match):
    a. understanding _____
    b. splendor _____
    c. foundation _____
    d. victory _____
    e. kingdom _____
    f. crown _____
    g. mercy _____
    h. wisdom _____
    i. beauty _____
    j. strength _____

SECTION 6

The Swirling Points of Energy—The Chakras

59. The word *chakra* comes from the Sanskrit word for
    a. wheel
    b. energy
    c. spirit
    d. light

60. The chakras are located
    a. along the spine
    b. along the spine and the hands and feet
    c. throughout the body
    d. in the upper body

61. The chakras are often depicted, especially in the Tantric system, as
    a. wheels
    b. lotus blossoms
    c. bright lights
    d. all of the above

62. The energy that moves up through the chakras is sometimes referred to as
    a. energy wheels
    b. the turtle
    c. magical threads
    d. the Kundalini snake

63. The element fire is associated with which chakra?
    a. solar plexus
    b. heart
    c. base of the spine/perineum
    d. top of the head

64. The element of water is associated with which chakra?
    a. heart
    b. throat
    c. lower abdomen
    d. forehead

65. One of the primary differences between working with the energy of the chakras for magical purposes versus strictly spiritual is
    a. in magic, the energy is contained and directed outward
    b. in magic, the energy is absorbed into the Witch
    c. the sexual charge generated in magical workings
    d. there is no difference between the two types of workings

66. Using this figure, match up each color with its corresponding chakra (1 point per match):

    a. indigo ____
    b. orange ____
    c. red   ____
    d. green ____
    e. yellow ____
    f. violet ____
    g. blue   ____

Answers to Chapter 6

Unless otherwise stated, give yourself *2 points for each correct answer.* At the end of the chapter, add together your totals from each section to get your final score for the chapter. This number will be carried forward to the end of the book for a final tally!

SECTION 1
Brushing the Dust off History

1. B.   Corpus Hermetica is attributed to Hermes Trismegistus, or "thrice great Hermes," a mythical alchemist who was said to be the grandson of Adam and a builder of the Egyptian pyramids. It consisted of forty-two sacred books, most of which have been lost, which contained the philosophy of the Egyptians, Priestly training, and teachings on the energies of elements, polarity, and self-transformation. With a strong emphasis on astrological and alchemical lore, much of modern magical practice and occult traditions, along with their symbolism, spells, and rituals, were influenced by Hermeticisim.

2. B.   He was also known as Abraham the Jew. Nicholas Flammel (1362–1460) bought these books, *The Sacred Magic of Abrameline the Mage,* from an unknown source. No one ever saw the book, but he described it at length. It was a major influence on modern magical orders. Originally in Hebrew, a purported French translation appeared in the eighteenth century and was later translated into English in the twentieth century. The manuscript contains information on the crafting of elaborate seals and sigils, the power of

numbers, sacred names, and rituals for conjuring spirits. It is said to been a major influence on both Crowley and Gardner.

For Further Reading: The Book of the Sacred Magic of Abra-Melin the Mage by MacGregor Mathers (Aquarian Press, 1976).

3. D. Born in 1493, Paracelsus became a philosopher and alchemist. He attempted to unite the mysticism of Nature with the Christian dogma. He longed for the elimination of the barriers between ritual practiced in and outside of the church. Paracelsus saw the entire cosmos in terms of a single entity, the Diva Matrix or divine womb of the Earth Mother. It is from Paracelsus that we get the Hermetic doctrine of "as above, so below," the concept that the Earth is a microcosm of the macrocosm of the universe.

4. D. Agrippa's full name was Henty Cornelius Agrippa von Nettesheim (1486–1535). His work *On Occult Philosophy* was a summation of all the magical and occult knowledge of the time. It had a major influence on practitioners of the occult and the development of Western esoteric thought. He argued that what was called magic was actually a natural psychic gift and had nothing to do with the devil. He believed that the connection between will and imagination can effect magic. He also believed that the highest potential for magic could be found within the balance of Nature.

5. C. Ceremonial Magicians viewed demons as powerful intelligences who can be summoned and controlled in rituals. Demons were invoked as a means to gain whatever it was that the Magician sought or needed: money, power, knowledge, or what have you. Although Magicians summoned and worked with demons, they did not consider themselves to be Satanists, because they were controlling—not worshiping or being controlled by—the demons. Magicians also work with other spirits, God forms, elementals, angels, and so forth. The Ceremonial Magician's circle is cast to protect the Magician. A small triangle is prepared outside the

Magician's circle in which the demon is conjured. Detailed methods for constructing these circles are found in the grimoires. It needs to be mentioned that while the older forms of Ceremonial Magic were highly influential upon the modern mystery and Western occult societies, the belief in, summoning of, or working with demons is *not* seen in modern practice.

6. B. John Dee (1527–1608) was a scholar with interest in the occult and magic. He and his partner, Edward Kelly, developed Enochian magic. Enochian is a language for calling or summoning spirits. It was made popular by Aleister Crowley in his work *Magic in Theory and Practice*. Present-day Enochian magic plays a role in the study of some modern Witches and other occultists.

7. D. Francis Barrett was an occultist and novelist with a strong interest in Ceremonial Magic and alchemy. It was Eliphas Lévi's interest in *The Magus* that brought it out of obscurity to became a major influence on twentieth-century occultists. Most unusual was that the book included an advertisement for students interested in the occult. It is believed that Barrett founded a school of magic in London, but no information on it or its activities have survived.

8. C. These books were reputed to have dated back to ancient sources. They were popular in the seventeenth through nineteenth centuries. The materials were said to have come from Hermetic texts dating back to 100 to 400 C.E.

9. B. The most famous of the grimoires is *The Key of Solomon*, which is supposed to have been written in the first century C.E. Over the years, it has been added to by various authors so that it is now impossible to ascertain what were the original parts of the text. A Greek version that dates back to 1100 to 1200 C.E. is at the British Museum. Much of the twentieth-century literature on Ceremonial Magic is derived from *The Key of Solomon*.

For Your Learning Enjoyment: Lemegeton is also called *The*

Lesser Key of Solomon. With claims of being a medieval magical text, the earliest reliable copies are actually only seventeenth century. It contains information on both white and black magic. *Grimoire of Honorius* was first published sometime between 1629 and 1670, and was popular during the seventeenth century. The text has a Christian base and is not considered an important magical book. *The Book of Black Magic and of Pacts* was published in 1898 by Arthur Edward Waite of Tarot card fame.

10. D. The most powerful of the names of power is Tetragrammaton, the name of the God of the Old Testament. It is usually expressed as YHWH—Yod, He, Vay, He. Aleister Crowley created AUGMN, an expansion of the Buddhist mantra *om,* as the ultimate word of power. Names of power are frequently associated with numeric formulas and other esoteric connections.

11. A. Eliphas Lévi put forth three laws of magic. First is the law of the power of will as an actual force. Magic is created through the summoned and directed power of the Magician's will. Second is the direction of the power of the astral light that is found within everything in the universe. And third, "as above, so below"—the concept that the microcosm and the macrocosm are reflections, and what happens within the micro can affect the macro.

    TOTAL YOUR POINTS
Chapter 6, section 1: Brushing the Dust off History

_____ Total number of questions 1–11 answered correctly

Multiply the total number of questions 1–11 answered correctly by 2. This will give you your total number of points for chapter 6, section 1:

$$\underline{\hspace{4cm}} \; X \, 2 = \; \underline{\hspace{4cm}}$$

Total number of questions 1–11   Total score, chapter 6,
answered correctly   section 1

Total possible points for chapter 6, section 1 = 22

SECTION 2

The Hermetic Order of the Golden Dawn

12. D. The key founder of the Hermetic Order of the Golden
Dawn was Dr. William Wynn Westcott. Westcott obtained,
or inherited, from a prominent mystic what appeared to be a
set of cipher manuscripts of Rosicrucian origin. Using his
Hermetic knowledge, he was able to translate the materials,
and discovered within them references to rituals for the
"Golden Dawn." He then asked MacGregor Mathers to
flesh out these rituals. From these translations and patches,
the five grades of the first order were formed. It was from
this material that the charter of the Golden Dawn was
based.

13. B. Isis-Urania temple was formed in London in 1888. It
was followed shortly by the Osiris temple at Weston-super-
Mare, Horus at Bradford, Amen-Ra in Edinburgh.

14. C. The original founders, Westcott, Mathers, Woodman,
and Woodford, were all members of the Rosicrucian Society.
Many of the members, most of whom came from the educated classes, were also involved with the Masons. Most of
the rituals were based largely on Freemasonry with Egyptian
and Greek imagery and drawing from Helena Blavatsky's
Isis Unveiled (1877).

15. C. A. E. Waite was a member of the Hermetic Order of the
Golden Dawn, but not until after the order had been in existence for a few years.

16. D. Gerald Gardner was never a member of the Golden

Dawn. Crowley belonged to the Golden Dawn from 1898 to 1903. His controversial membership in the Golden Dawn has been pointed to as one of the reasons the organization splintered, did make Gardner an honorary member of the O.T.O. Crowley possibly gave him materials that he had acquired during his time with the Golden Dawn, which Gardner then used in his own practices.

17. A.   There are three orders: the Outer Order, Second Order, and Third Order. There are ten grades, not counting the neophyte. Each grade corresponds with a sephiroth on the Tree of Life of the Kabbalah.

For Your Learning Enjoyment: The First Order, or Outer Order, consists of Neophyte, Zelator, Theoricus, Practicus, Philosophus. The Second Order begins with the grade Adeptus Minor, which is broken down into Adeptus Zelator, Adeptus Theoricus, Adeptus Practicus, and Adeptus Philosophus. Adeptus Major and Adeptus Extemptus are the other two degrees within this grade. The Third Order consists of Magister Templi, Magus, Ipsissmus.

18. D.   The degrees of Third Order cannot be obtained while in the body; they are conveyed in the spirit realms . . . meaning you have to be dead, or noncoporeal.

19. D.   Wiccan Traditions owe a lot to the Golden Dawn, including the concept of assuming God forms, the concept of the Watchtowers, our elemental attributes and color associations, our ritual tools, and the Tarot in its modern form.

For More Information: The Golden Dawn, as revealed by Israel Regardie (Llewellyn Publications, 1988).

 TOTAL YOUR POINTS
Chapter 6, section 2: Hermetic Order of the Golden Dawn

_____ Total number of questions 12–19 answered correctly

Multiply the total number of questions 12–19 answered correctly by 2. This will give you your total number of points for chapter 6, section 2:

_____ X 2 = _____
Total number of questions 12–19   Total score, chapter 6,
answered correctly   section 2

Total possible points for chapter 6, section 2 = 16

SECTION 3

Cloaked in Secrecy—Influential Magical Societies

20. C. The Ordo Templi Orientis was founded in 1902 by Karl Kellner. It combines elements of Oriental and European Tantrism.

21. D. Tantra or Esoteric Buddhism is a form of Tibetan Buddhism that combines Tibetan folk religion, Shamanism, and divination. In Tantra, sexual imagery represents the ecstatic union of opposites and connection with the Divine. The practice of Tantra aids in the development of psychic powers. Sex magic takes this one step farther by using this ecstatic and psychic energy. This was one of the key focuses in the O.T.O. Tradition.

22. D. Mysteria Mystica Maxima was the name of his chapter. Crowley met Theodore Reuss, the head of the German O.T.O., in 1912. Crowley then established the English branch of the organization that same year.

    For Your Learning Enjoyment: Roseae Rubeae et Aureae Crucis is the name of the Second Order of the Hermetic Order of the Golden Dawn. It was introduced in 1892. Alpha et Omega and Stella Matutina were among the splinter groups founded after the breakup of the Golden Dawn. Stella Matutina was regrouped by A. E. Waite around the Isis-Urania Temple of the Golden Dawn. J. W. Brodie-Innes founded the Alpha et Omega in London.

23. C. Only those with a rank of Master Freemason need apply! Membership was limited to those who achieved the rank of Master Masons who also professed a belief in Christian doctrine. Membership in the Rosicrucian Society was a prerequisite for entry into a number of other occult societies around the turn of the twentieth century.

24. C. With the above requirements, it should come as no surprise that the principles of the society included Gnosticism applied to Christian doctrine combined with alchemic and esoteric studies.

25. B. Helena Blavatsky was a Russian spiritualist and clairvoyant. She, along with Colonel H. S. Olcott, created the Theosophical Society in New York City in 1875. He became president upon her death in 1891. The society moved its headquarters in 1877 to India.

26. B. Helena Blavatsky was a Russian spiritualist and clairvoyant. She published *Isis Unveiled* in 1877. It is a combination of Hindu, Buddhist, Gnostic, and Kabbalistic concepts. The Hermetic Order of the Golden Dawn drew from this work when forming their rituals.

    For Your Learning Enjoyment: Foundations of Practical Magic: An Introduction to Qabalistic, Magical and Meditative Techniques is by Israel Regardie (Aquarian Press, 1979). *Portable Darkness* is an Aleister Crowley reader edited by Scott Michaelsen (Harmony Books, 1989). *The Magus* was written by Francis Barrett.

27. D. Israel Regardie was an occultist who became friends with and secretary to Aleister Crowley. In 1934, he was initiated into Stella Matutina, a magical order derived from the ashes of the Hermetic Order of the Golden Dawn, which had collapsed in 1903. He published the teachings of the Golden Dawn in 1937, breaking his oath but making the materials available to generations of Witches and Pagans. In the early 1980s, he began training initiates. They went on to reconstitute the Hermetic Order of the Golden Dawn.

For Your Learning Enjoyment: Scott Michaelsen is the editor of *Portable Darkness,* an Aleister Crowley reader (Harmony Books, 1989). Aidan Kelly wrote *Crafting the Art of Magic: A History of Modern Witchcraft 1939–1964* (Llewellyn, 1991). Jack L. Bracelin was Gardner's secretary and the author of Gardner's biography, *Witch.*

28. D. Aleister Crowley (1875–1947) was a controversial but talented and influential occultist of the twentieth century. Supposedly, in April 1904 a being who called itself Aiwass made itself known to Crowley. For three days he appeared, bidding Crowley to write down what was being dictated to him. These transcriptions are known as the Liber Al vel Legis, the so-called *Book of the Law.*

29. A. The Law of Thelema was included in the Liber Al vel Legis. It is believed that Crowley received the Law of Thelema from some other source; still, he is often credited with having written what many have called the beginnings of the Wiccan Rede.

30. A. The north is the place of dark and mystery. The focus of the Masons is completely on the light, therefore the east, south, and west quarters are the places of importance, while nothing stands or occupies in the northern realm. Witches, however, often place their altars in the north for this very reason!

31. D. Annie Besant founded the British Co-Masons, a group that is open to both men and women. Gerald Gardner was initiated into this Co-Masonic order. Besant was also a member of the Rosicrucian Fellowship of Crotona, the group that was reportedly a cover for the New Forest Coven.

32. D. Many Wiccans, if attending a Masonic ritual, would be shocked at the numbers of ritual elements and vocabulary terms that would be familiar to them. Many aspects of modern Wiccan ritual were taken directly from the Masons. Those listed are just a few. Elemental associations, however, come from the Golden Dawn.

<u>TOTAL YOUR POINTS</u>
Chapter 6, section 3: nfluential Magical Societies

_____ Total number of questions 20–32 answered correctly

Multiply the total number of questions 20–32 answered correctly by 2. This will give you your total number of points for chapter 6, section 3:

_____ X 2 = _____

Total number of questions 20–32   Total score, chapter 6,
answered correctly   section 3

Total possible points for chapter 6, section 3 = 26

SECTION 4
Working With Angels—Ceremonial Magic

33. C. Knowledge, to know, to seek out inner wisdom. The courage, to dare, to challenge preconceptions. To will, to have the strength to stay focused on your path and on your working. Silence, to speak of things only that can be spoken of and to listen in the quiet to hear your inner voice.

34. C. A lamen is a large symbol worn on a chain around the neck so that it falls on the breast. It can be made of anything from metal to colored cardboard. Lamens represent the office of those who wear them, are symbols of the deities, act as talismans, and also accumulate a magical charge during ritual. For these reasons, lamens are treated with respect and are not removed from the temple.

35. B. Jachin and Boaz; mercy and judgment. They represent the two points of polar opposites and balance: male and female, positive and negative, construction and destruction. They stand representing the gateway to knowledge.

36. A. The left side.

37. C. The Lesser Banishing Ritual is one of the essential rituals of the Occult Western Mysteries observed by Hermeticists. Forces are summoned to purify the space within the magic circle to guard it against interference and to empower the Magician.

38. A. A decagon is a geometric figure made up of ten triangles that unite at the apexes to form a ten-sided polygon. Pythagoras considered it the symbol of the universe.

39. A. Air.

40. C. Water.

41. D. Earth.

42. B. Fire.

43. D. Samuel is an angel, but not one invoked as part of the Lesser Ritual of the Pentagram.

44. C. Michael is at your right hand.
    For Your Learning Enjoyment: Raphael is before me, Gabriel behind me, Michael at my right hand, and Auriel at my left.

45. B. Sulfur, mercury, salt.

46. The Four Holy Creatures or Kerubs depicted in religious art are the Man, the Lion, the Eagle, and the Bull. Each is also associated with one of the four Evangelists: Matthew is the Man, Mark the Lion, John the Eagle, and Luke the Bull.

a.	Lion	3	fire—Leo
b.	Bull	1	earth—Taurus
c.	Man	2	air—Aquarius
d.	Eagle	4	water—Scorpio

47. Match up each metal with its corresponding planet in alchemy:

a. lead	5	Saturn
b. tin	3	Jupiter
c. iron	1	Mars
d. gold	7	sun
e. copper/brass	2	Venus
f. quicksilver	6	Mercury
g. silver	4	moon

 ## TOTAL YOUR SCORE
Chapter 6, section 4: Working With Angels—Ceremonial Magic

_____ Total number of questions 33–45 answered correctly

Multiply this total by 2:

_____ X 2 = _____
Total number of 2-point questions   Total 2-point questions,
33–45 answered correctly   chapter 6, section 4

Total your 1-point matches:

_____ Total number of 1-point matches, question 46
+ _____ Total number of 1-point matches, question 47
= _____

Add together your 2-point total with your 1-point total:

_____   +   _____   =   _____
1-point total   2-point total   Total score, chapter
                                                              6, section 4

Total possible points for chapter 6, section 4 = 37

For More Information: The Ritual Magic Workbook by Dolores Ashcroft-Nowicki (Aquarian Press, 1986).

SECTION 5

Climbing the Tree of Life—The Kabbalah

48. B. There are ten sephiroth.

49. C. There are thirty-two paths of wisdom—twenty-two paths that connect the sephiroth *plus* the ten sephiroth themselves.

50. C. There are five sephiroth on the middle pillar: Malkuth, Yesod, Tiphareth, Da'ath, and Kether.

51. B. There are four worlds of the Kabbalah, each corresponding with one of the four letters of God: Yod, He, Vav, He. The Tree is the same in all four worlds, but the powers expressed are different in each of the worlds. Each realm increases in form until you reach the last world, which is the one we exist in—or at least *most* of us do—where it is so dense we can't see beyond ourselves. These worlds exist simultaneously, each reflecting a different level of existence of being.

52. A. The left pillar is the pillar of severity. The center is the pillar of mildness. The right is the pillar of mercy.

53. D. Assiah is the fourth and lowest world. Being the lowest, it is, of course, where we live. It represents the physical world or substance.
    For Your Learning Enjoyment: Starting from the top and working down to where we grovel: Atziluth is the first world. It is the realm of the spiritual, of Divine Archetypes or deity energy—in other words, where the Gods live. Briah is the second world, the archangelic world of creations and of emotions. Yetzirah is the angelic world of thought and formation.

54. B. Da'ath is between Tiphareth and Kether. It is the empty sephiroth, the abyss. It is sometimes represented by the number 0. It is not a true sephiroth but more the absence of

one. It is said that this place was where Malkuth, the tenth sephiroth found at the base of the Tree, used to reside before its fall to the earthly realms. *Da'ath* means "gnosis" or "knowledge." It isn't a sphere of light and is usually drawn as a dotted circle.

55. B. The kingdom is located at the bottom of the Tree of Life!

56. A. The sephiroth Yesod is associated with the element air and is considered the foundation of manifestation. You've got to be able to think it before it can become reality.

57. Match up each sephiroth with its name (1 point per correct match!):

a.	Thiphareth	6
b.	Yesod	9
c.	Chokmah	2
d.	Netzach	7
e.	Chesed	4
f.	Geburah	5
g.	Hod	8
h.	Kether	1
i.	Malkuth	10
j.	Binah	3

58. Match up each sephiroth with its corresponding attribute (1 point per match!):

a.	understanding	3
b	splendor	8
c.	foundation	9
d.	victory	7
e.	kingdom	10
f.	crown	1
g.	mercy	4
h.	wisdom	2
i.	beauty	6
j.	strength	5

For More Information: The Witches Tarot by Ellen Cannon Reed (Llewellyn, 1990). *The Mystical Qabalah* by Dion Fortune (Weiser, 1984). *The Shining Paths: An Experiential Journey Through the Tree of Life* by Dolores Ashcroft-Nowicki (Aquarian Press, 1983).

TOTAL YOUR POINTS
Chapter 6, section 5: Climbing the Tree of Life—The Kabbalah

_____ Total number of questions 48–56 answered correctly

Multiply the total number of questions 48–56 answered correctly by 2:

_____ X 2 = _____

Total number of questions   Total 2-point questions,
48–56 answered correctly   chapter 6, section 5

_____ Total number of 1-point matches, question 57
+ _____ Total number of 1-point matches, question 58
= _____

Add together your 2-point total with your 1-point total:

_____ + _____ = _____

1-point total,   2-point total,   Total score, chapter
questions 57   questions 48–56   6, section 5
and 58

Total possible points for chapter 6, section 5 = 38

SECTION 6

The Swirling Points of Energy—The Chakras

59. A. The word *chakra* comes from the Sanskrit word for "wheel." It also reflects where this system of energy work comes to us—Eastern mysticism.

60. C. The chakras are energy centers that are actually located throughout your entire body. Those individuals who use their hands or feet a lot, especially for healing work, probably already recognize the power centers located in those areas! The major chakras, and the ones most worked with, are found running from the base of your spine to the top, or crown, of your head. Energy is drawn into your body and used through these centers.

61. B. The chakras are often depicted as many-petaled lotus flowers, the number of petals varying per chakra.

62. D. It is said that the Kundalini snake lives at the base of the spine, where it sits curled up around the first chakra, waiting to be awakened. It is a powerful force once all the chakras have been awakened and the snake moves freely through them. Some people associate the movement with sexual energy.

63. A. The solar plexus is associated with the element fire.
     For Your Learning Enjoyment: The heart is the home of air in the chakra system. Earth is found at the first chakra, the closest to the Earth itself, the base of your spine. The top of your head is the Crone with no real elemental association, but it is coupled with thought.

64. C. The lower abdomen, otherwise known as the womb, is connected with the element water.
     For Your Learning Enjoyment: The throat is coupled with ether or sound. The heart, as previously mentioned, is air. The forehead has no elemental association but is connected with light in the chakra system.

65. A. Magic is the art of creating change. In magical practices, the energy generated and raised within the chakras is focused and directed outward for a purpose. For example, the energy charge would be sent out to aid in the healing of another person. When used within traditional Eastern spiritual practices, the energy is raised and drawn up through each of the chakras until it reaches the crown, where it expands to create a connection and union with the Divine, also known as the point of enlightenment.

66. Using the figure on page 252, match up each color with its corresponding chakra (1 point per match):

   a. indigo   _6_
   b. orange   _2_
   c. red   _1_
   d. green   _4_
   e. yellow   _3_
   f. violet   _7_
   g. blue   _5_

 TOTAL YOUR POINTS
Chapter 6, section 6: The Swirling Points of Energy—The Chakras

_____ Total number of questions 59–66 answered correctly

Multiply the total number of questions 31–65 answered correctly by 2:

_____ X 2 = _____
Total number of questions 59–65   Total 2-point questions,
answered correctly   chapter 6, section 6

+ _____ Total number of 1-point matches, question 66

= _____

Add together your 2-point total with your 1-point total:

_____   +   _____   =   _____

1-point total,   2-point total   Total score, chapter 6,
question 66   questions 59–64   section 6

Total possible points for chapter 6, section 6 = 21

TOTALING CHAPTER 6

Add together your final scores from each section in chapter 6:

_____ Chapter 6, section 1—Brushing the Dust off History
+ _____ Chapter 6, section 2—Hermetic Order of the Golden Dawn
+ _____ Chapter 6, section 3—Influential Magical Societies
+ _____ Chapter 6, section 4—Ceremonial Magic
+ _____ Chapter 6, section 5—The Kabbalah
+ _____ Chapter 6, section 6—The Chakras

= [____] Grand total for chapter 6

This is the number you will carry forward to the end of the book!

Total possible points for chapter 6 = 160

7

Putting It Together
What Is Your Wicca I.Q.?

Congratulations on completing the quiz! It was a lot of material to work through, and no matter how well or poorly you did, you should be proud of yourself. Remember, this book is a tool for identifying areas of strength and pinpointing those you may want to develop. No matter what your score, remember that life is a classroom and we are always learning!

Tally the Totals

Now comes the moment of truth. Add together your grand totals from each of the chapters:

_____ Chapter 1: You Believe What?!
+ _____ Chapter 2: Tools of the Trade
+ _____ Chapter 3: Which Witch Is Which?
+ _____ Chapter 4: Burn Two Candles and Call Me in the Morning
+ _____ Chapter 5: Unraveling Entrails
+ _____ Chapter 6: Cerebellum Ceremonium
_____ Your Wicca I.Q.!

Final Assessment

Disclaimer: *Although the following assessment is based on traditional coven titles, this book* cannot *confer any actual degree! Degrees can only be bestowed by the Gods or earned through a Tradition with a degree system.*

0–307: Dedicant

Your toes are on the path, but you really haven't a clue. You may be feeling a bit overwhelmed and intimidated right now. Don't be discouraged—we all had to begin somewhere! No Witch started off intuitively knowing everything.

A Dedicant is someone who has made a heart pledge to explore the possibilities and to see whether Wicca is actually the right path to be walking. Your first step should be to start with the basics. I suggest looking over the bibliography at the end of this book and identifying a couple of general books for further reading. In addition, pick *one* topic—for example, mythology or runes—in an area that you did poorly on in the quiz but in which you also have an interest. Find two books on that *one* topic and read them. I'm emphasizing *one topic* because it's so easy to get bogged down if you try to become competent in many areas all at once. Two books make a good starting point, because they will provide you with two different insights—no two authors view the same subject matter the same way. But choose only two to begin with, because having too many authors at the beginning of study is like having too many chefs in the kitchen. They get into each other's way and confusion occurs!

Also look around you for your Wiccan and Pagan community. Most areas have a Pagan or occult store where information on community events can be found. If you haven't a store in your area, try the Internet. There are a number of groups listed online, some of which offer public events or gatherings. And now comes the warning label . . . *always* be cautious when attending or meeting any group for the first time. We may all be Gods and Goddesses, but some deities are not the most scrupulous of entities. Look at Loki, the Norse trickster God! If a group makes you feel uncomfortable, *leave*. If someone tries to force you to do something that raises serious moral or ethical questions, don't do it. While some covens will ask for funds to help defray the cost of ritual supplies, if large sums of money are required for study, be concerned. If a group revolves around a charismatic leader who is insisting that you must sever all ties with friends and family—*run!* What it boils down to is that there are thousands of Traditions and covens all over the world. Pick the groups in which you enjoy spending time. The same goes if you decide to join a coven. Joining a coven is like joining a family. Take your time and be very picky.

Dedicant, as you explore, keep in mind that the answer to whether *Am I meant to walk this path?* might be, *no*. Even if that is the case, because knowledge has a way of altering our perceptions by expanding our vision, what you have learned during your exploration will forever change you. If you find that Wicca is not your religious calling, go with peace and may your feet lead you home. But if the answer is *yes*, then welcome to your journey. May you find happiness and joy.

308–676: First Degree

Your feet are firmly on the path, but you've got a long way to go! You, too, may be feeling a bit overwhelmed by all the information presented. So much to know! But take heart—knowledge comes with time and practice.

Your first step is to go back over this test, list those areas within each chapter that you scored high in, and compare them with areas where you did poorly. Do you notice a trend? Some parts of this book involve purely intellectual matters, while others are more intuitive. If you scored high in sections such as mythology, ancient history, or Ceremonial Magic, then you've been spending too much time with your nose in a book and not enough outside with Nature. This is an experiential religion—get out there and meet a few people and tree spirits! On the other hand, if you did well in the chapters on the circle, divination, or spellcraft, then perhaps it's time to go back and do a little more research.

677–1046: *Second Degree, Priest or Priestess of the Craft*

Congratulations—you have an excellent grasp on many aspects of the Wiccan religion and practices. You know your stuff! Now it's time to fine-tune and fill in the gaps.

Have you been focusing too much on the beliefs of Wicca and not enough on the practice? Are you strong in Hermetics but weak in divination? Many people taking this test have been practicing for years but still will not receive a high score in every section . . . or perhaps even in *any* area. That's okay. Many Traditions don't emphasize all the different aspects presented in this book.

Perhaps this quiz uncovered a few weaknesses you didn't know you had and surprised you by showing you that you know more on some topics than you thought you did. May you enjoy your continued walk along the path. I hope this book has given you some insights and ideas on directions to go for further study or areas to brush up on.

After all, life is a continual growth process. Wicca is not about where you are but about where you are going. Just make sure to have some fun along the way.

1049–1234: *Third Degree, High Priest or Priestess of the Old Religion*

Are you sure you didn't cheat? Well then, congratulations— you made it! You've got a solid understanding of the wide breadth and deep knowledge of our Craft. Pass on the knowledge and keep learning! *(Reminder: Reaching this level does not confer an actual title or degree! These can only be bestowed by the Gods or earned through a Tradition with a degree system.)*

Tools for Evaluating Each Chapter

For those of you who wish to see how well you did within each chapter, here is a simple assessment. The individual chapter totals are as follows:

Chapter One:	230
Chapter Two:	208
Chapter Three:	228
Chapter Four:	216
Chapter Five:	190
Chapter Six:	160
TOTAL	1232

Evaluation for Chapters

Chapter One
Dedicant:	0–56
First	57–125
Second	126–194
Third	195–230

Chapter Two
Dedicant	1–51
First	52–113
Second	114–175
Third	176–208

Chapter Three
Dedicant	1–56
First	57–124
Second	125–192
Third	193–228

Chapter Four
   Dedicant   0–53
   First   54–117
   Second   118–182
   Third   183–216

Chapter Five
   Dedicant   0–46
   First   47–103
   Second   104–161
   Third   162–190

Chapter 6
   Dedicant   0–31
   First   32–87
   Second   88–135
   Third   136–160

Want more *What's Your Wicca I.Q.?*
     See www.LauraWildman.net

Bibliography

Buckland, Raymond. *Buckland's Complete Book of Witchcraft*. St. Paul, Minnesota. Llewllyn Publications, 1995.

Conway, D.J. *The Ancient and Shining Ones, World Myth, Magic and Religion*. St. Paul, Minnesota, Llewellyn Publications, 1994.

Ferguson, Diana. *The Magickal Year*. New York, N.Y. Labyrinth Publishing, UK, 1996.

Frazer, Sir James George. *The Golden Bough, the Roots of Religion and Folklore,* two volumes in one. New York, NY. Avenel Books, 1981.

Guiley, Rosemary Ellen. *The Encyclopedia of Witches & Witchcraft, 2ⁿᵈ Edition,* New York, Checkmark Books, 1999.

Hutton, Ronald. *Triumph of the Moon, a History of Modern Pagan Witchcraft*. Oxford, England. Oxford University Press, 1999.

Jordan, Michael. *Witches, and Encyclopedia of Paganism and Magic*. London, England, Kyle Cathie Limited, 1998.

Jordan, Michael. *Encyclopedia of Gods, over 2500 Deities of the World*. New York, Facts of File Inc., 1993.

Regardie, Israel. *What You Should Know About the Golden Dawn*. Phoenix, Arizona. Falcon Press, 1987.

Valiente, Doreen. *The Rebirth of Witchcraft*. Custer, Washington. Phoenix Publishing, 1989.

Zimmerman, Denise & Gleason, Katherine A. *The Idiots Guide to Wicca and Witchcraft*. Indianapolis, Indiana. Alpha Books, 2000.

About the Author

Laura Wildman is a Third Degree Gardnerian Witch trained in the Protean tradition. Along with organizing and participating in hundreds of rituals and workshops since 1985, she has lectured and taught classes on Wicca for more than fifteen years and is a legally recognized Wiccan clergy in her home state of Massachusetts. Laura is also a faculty member and chair of the Interfaith Development and Community Rites of Passage Department at Cherry Hill Seminary, a Pagan seminary located in Vermont.

Laura is the cofounder of the original *New Moon,* a Pagan networking organization in the Boston area. She is also one of the founders of *New Moon New York* and *New Moon in the Valley,* which are branches of this same organization. *New Moon* is a nonprofit Pagan networking organization. It serves those people whose religious focus is polytheistic or Nature-centered. *New Moon* acts as an interfaith group, bringing together any and all on spiritually life-affirming paths for the purpose of sharing knowledge and making social connections.

Laura lives in western Massachusetts with her husband, Tom, and their Maltese dogs, Lady Clandora and Lord Titan. She is the High Priestess of the Apple and Oak Coven, and active in the Covenant of the Goddess local chapter, Weavers CoG.